T0085790

Advance Praise for *Girl to Boss!*

"*Girl to Boss!: Advice for Girls from 50 of America's Most Successful Women* by Julia Taylor Brandus (with a little help from Mom and Dad) is a great resource for the next generation of women leaders. The collection of conversations helps young women dream big by providing impactful stories, thoughtful advice, and tangible lessons all from the perspective of ten-year-old Julia Taylor Brandus. Interviewees include prominent leaders from a broad range of industries—artificial intelligence, business, sustainability, government, technology, and more—a testament to the boundless possibilities of women. I am confident this book will serve to empower and inspire the next generation of women leaders."

—Jessica Sibley, CEO, Time Inc.

Girl to BOSS

Advice for Girls from 50 of
America's Most Successful Women

Julia Taylor Brandus
with help from Dad, Paul Brandus

A POST HILL PRESS BOOK
ISBN: 978-1-63758-993-9
ISBN (eBook): 978-1-63758-994-6

Post Hill Press
New York • Nashville
posthillpress.com

Published in the United States of America
2 3 4 5 6 7 8 9 10

To my mom and dad, who helped me with this book. I would also like to dedicate it to my Grandma Roro, and to my Grandpa Gene, Grandpa Papa, and Grandma Nana, who are watching from the heavens.

Table of Contents

Foreword xiii

A Note from Julia and Her Dad 1

Artificial Intelligence

Elizabeth "Beth" Ballard: Engineer, Argo AI 6

Megan McConnell: Artificial Intelligence Consultant,
McKinsey & Co. 10

Aviation and Aerospace

Julia Cline: Research Aerospace Engineer, NASA Langley
Research Center 16

Betsy MacLennan: Pilot, First Officer, United Airlines 22

Biotechnology and Pharmaceutical

Pam Randhawa: Chief Executive Officer, Emperiko Corp. 28

Blockchain, Crypto, and Digital Currencies

Amy Kim: Policy Lead for Blockchain, Crypto, and Digital
Currencies, PayPal Inc. 36

Cybersecurity

Leslie Anderson: Chief Strategist, Cybersecurity Operations,
MITRE Corp. 42

Data Science

Janet Jones-Oliveira: Data Scientist and Director of Advanced
Technology, Verite Group, Inc. 46

Economics, Finance, and Venture Capital

Marguerita Cheng, CFP: Chief Executive Officer, Blue Ocean
Global Wealth 54

Schelo Doirin: Founder, Black Women Invest 58

Constance Hunter: Economist, Executive Vice President, Global
Head of Strategy and ESG (Environmental, Social, and
Governance), American International Group, Inc. 63

Esther Lee: Chief Executive Officer, Refraction 68

Kimberly Smith Spacek: Head of Capital Formation,
TechStars 71

Education

Ruth Ben-Ghiat: Professor, New York University; Historian,
Author, and Commentator 78

Gail Helt: Assistant Professor of Political Science, Director of
the King Security and Intelligence Studies, King University;
former Central Intelligence Agency officer 82

Dr. Anne Kress: President, Northern Virginia Community
College 86

Lauren Strawderman: Third-Grade Teacher 91

Energy

Noël Bakhtian: Director of Tech Acceleration, Bezos
Earth Fund 96

Mei Cai: Director, Battery Cell Systems Research, General Motors
Research & Development 100

Environment and Sustainability

Amy Berry: Chief Executive Officer, Tahoe Fund 106

Cora Snyder: Senior Researcher, Pacific Institute 111

Government Service

Carmela Conroy: Foreign Service Officer (ret.), U.S. Department
of State; Democratic Party Chair 116

Carmen Medina: Deputy Director, Central Intelligence Agency
(ret.); Co-Author, *Rebels at Work: A Handbook for Leading
Change from Within* 120

Ileana Ros-Lehtinen: Fifteen-Term Congresswoman from Florida
(1989–2019); Senior Advisor on Public Policy, Akin Gump
Strauss Hauer & Feld 124

Journalism

Maureen Dowd: Pulitzer Prize–Winning Columnist, *The New York Times* 130

Norah O'Donnell: Anchor, *CBS Evening News* 135

Legal and Law Enforcement

Jill Baker: Criminal Defense Attorney, Minnesota Judicial Branch, Fifth Judicial District 142

Subhashini Bollini: Civil Rights Attorney, Partner, Correia & Puth, PLLC 147

Susan Friedlander: Earman General District Court Judge 153

Stacey Kincaid: Sheriff 158

Marketing

Kathryne Reeves: Chief Marketing Officer, Illumina, Inc. 164

Media, Arts, and Entertainment

Emily Greenspan: Owner, Tag-Arts, and Art Consultant 172

Eun Sun Kim: Music Director, San Francisco Opera 176

Jill Hennessy: Actor, Singer, Songwriter 180

Margaret Wallace: Entrepreneur, Gaming and Media Professional, Co-Founder of Playmatics; Professor, Boston University.....184

Medicine and Healthcare

Dr. Rina Bansal, MD: MBA President, Inova Alexandria Hospital 190

Jean Braden: Nurse Practitioner, The Children's Clinic 195

Dr. Sandy Ibrahim: Primary Care Physician, Medical Director at Inova 360° Concierge Medicine 200

Dr. Seema Yasmin: Epidemiologist, Stanford University; Professor, University of California, Los Angeles; Journalist 204

Military

Vernice "Flygirl" Armour: America's First Black Female Combat Pilot, First Black Female Pilot in the U.S. Marine Corps, Entrepreneur, Investor, Police Officer, Keynote Speaker 212

Philanthropy

Cynthia Germanotta (Lady Gaga's Mom): President, Born This
Way Foundation 220

Risk Management

Meredith Wilson: Chief Executive Officer, Emergent Risk
International 228

Sports

Cynthia Marshall: Chief Executive Officer, Dallas Mavericks,
National Basketball Association 234

Benita Fitzgerald Mosley: Olympic Gold Medalist; Vice
President, Community & Impact, and President, FundPlay,
LeagueApps 240

Technology and Software

Jeanette Cajide: Vice President of Strategy, Dialexa (an IBM
company) 246

Jakita Owensby Thomas: Phillpott Westpoint Stevens
Distinguished Professor of Computer Science and Software
Engineering, Auburn University 250

Tonya Walley: Vice President of Field Operations Strategy, Cox
Communications 254

Transportation

Diana Marina Cooper: Global Head of Policy & Regulations,
Supernal 262

Travel and Tourism

Kristin Kitchen: Chief Executive Officer, Sojourn Heritage
Accommodations 268

Veterinary and Animal Care

Dr. Molly Benner: Veterinarian 276

Profile Index 281
About the Author 283

Foreword

There has perhaps been no better time than now for this uplifting and inspiring book, *Girl to Boss!: Advice for Girls from 50 of America's Most Successful Women.* The author, Julia Brandus, age eleven, with the help of her dad—Paul Brandus, a presidential historian and author—spent eighteen months interviewing fifty groundbreaking women from all walks of life and disparate backgrounds. The result? A bountiful roadmap of how to find your girl-power to become your own girl to boss!

In this essential message, you will find that a boss can take on many different forms and serve numerous roles in society. And while the women interviewed have varied accomplishments, they each share one common denominator: they dreamed big and never let anyone talk them out of fulfilling their dreams. By ignoring the noise and focusing on finding your joy and your passion, you too can find yourself and your true calling.

You will learn firsthand from this book that while the journey may be difficult, if you concentrate on being your best self, the possibilities are limitless. Remember, you deserve that seat at the table—even if your seat is the only one occupied by a female. Remind yourself, it is leaders like those showcased in this book who created the path that girls like you get to follow. Enjoy the read! And then set out to create your own pathway that others can follow!

Maria E. Brennan
President & CEO The WICT Network:
Empowering Women in Media,
Entertainment & Technology

A Note from Julia and Her Dad

In the summer of 2021, my then nine-year-old daughter, Julia, came to me and asked, "How can I write a book like you?" (I've been fortunate to have written a few). I told her we should do something challenging and inspiring. This book is the result.

I explained to Julia that more than half the U.S. population is women, according to the 2020 Census. And yet:

- Only 28 percent of the 118th Congress are women (153 of 540 voting and nonvoting members).[1]
- Only 24 percent of governors are women (twelve of fifty).
- Only 10 percent of S&P 500 companies have a woman chief executive officer (thirty-three of 500).[2]
- Women represented just 14 percent of solo startup founders in 2021[3] and received just 2.1 percent of the venture capital (VC) deployed in 2022[4]

- Women represent just 13 percent of U.S. patent owners.[5]
- In so-called "STEM" jobs—Science, Technology, Engineering, and Math—which cover fields such as life sciences, agriculture, and environmental sciences, physical and earth sciences, engineering and architecture, computer and information sciences, math and statistics, and health-related fields—the overall representation of women remains disproportionately low.

For Black and Hispanic women, all of this data is even more discouraging.[6]

You get the idea. These figures should be higher! We want more women in Congress and in statehouses around the country. We want more women CEOs. More women starting companies, raising capital, taking chances—and reaping the rewards.

Girls everywhere should know of the enormous opportunities that lie on the horizon. Girls who will be going to college soon, entering the workforce, and hopefully changing our country. Girls to Bosses.

So Julia set out—with a bit of guidance from me—to interview fifty amazing, successful women. Women whose stories and advice will inspire girls everywhere. Girls who became bosses. CEOs. Members of Congress. Scientists.

Spies. Olympic gold medalists. Diplomats. Pulitzer Prize-winning journalists. Venture capitalists. And more.

We hope you'll enjoy *Girl to Boss!*—and also check out our pages on Instagram, TikTok, and YouTube. And email me (Julia) anytime—I would love to hear from you! My email is GirlToBoss@gmail.com.

Julia Brandes

Paul Brandes

Artificial Intelligence

now

THEN

Elizabeth "Beth" Ballard

Engineer, Argo AI (self-driving vehicles)

📍 Pittsburgh, Pennsylvania

Cars that can drive themselves?
It's the future!

Hello! You are a hardware engineer at Argo. What is Argo? What does a hardware engineer do? Please tell me about your job.

Argo AI is an independent self-driving technology platform company. We build the software, hardware, maps, and cloud-support infrastructure to power self-driving vehicles. Our technology will enable autonomous commercial services for delivering goods, hailing rides, and more.

Hardware engineers at Argo are responsible for the development of the sensing and computing modules for this, and the integration of those modules onto vehicle platforms.

My role at Argo is Vehicle Interfaces Manager. My team's responsibilities include component positioning, structural integration, cooling systems, cleaning systems, and more. Our work starts with detailed analysis and requirement definition, progresses through core design engineering, and concludes with validation and verification. My role in managing the team is to set technical direction for the team and enable their success in delivering high-performing designs.

What skills are the most important for you to know to do your job?

Communication is a key to every part of my job. Whether it's communicating with my team, external partners, parts suppliers or customers, or Argo's leadership, efficient communication is absolutely critical.

Critical thinking is also very important. This comes into play in a variety of ways. One is in evaluating risk in a project or design so we can further analyze or test it to address that risk. Another is in setting priorities. Time is always limited, so careful thinking through what is most important to spend time on is a key to success.

What do you like best about your job?

What I like best about my job is being challenged every day. Whether the challenge is in managing my team, growing my technical expertise, collaborating with peers, or something else, there is something new to learn and opportunities to grow through the experiences.

What did you study in college, and where did you go?

I studied Mechanical Engineering at Pennsylvania State University.

What do you know now that you wish you had known at age ten?

I wish at age ten I realized how important it is to learn to work with people from all different cultures, backgrounds, etc. and how enjoyable it is.

What is the one best piece of advice you have for young girls who will be going to high school, college, and joining the workforce in the next decade or so?

Don't sell yourself short. Challenge yourself and believe in yourself. Don't stay with what feels comfortable or safe. Set your dreams high and pursue them. Apply for the organization, school, or job you want even if you don't know if you are qualified, and put forth your best effort toward it.

Is there a quote, an inspirational thought, or anything like that that motivates you each day?

I really like the quote "Find a job you enjoy doing, and you will never have to work a day in your life." I don't fully believe that some days won't still feel like "work," but to me, enjoying my job makes life much more enjoyable.

Can you tell me about a professional or personal setback you had, how you overcame it, and what you learned from it?

My first job out of college I was given a quality engineering role, which was not where I wanted my career to lead. I overcame this by putting forth my best effort toward the job as well as immediately beginning to network and making my interest in R&D (research and development) known to my managers and others for consideration for my next position. I learned it is very important to do your best work even when it is not what you want to be doing. If those I was looking to work with in the future did not see me doing well in my first role, they likely would not have wanted me on their team to allow me that opportunity. I also learned the value of networking to open up opportunities.

> **"Find a job you enjoy doing, and you will never have to work a day in your life."**
>
> **—Often attributed to the likes of Mark Twain and Confucius**

now

THEN

Megan McConnell

 Artificial Intelligence Consultant, McKinsey & Co.

📍 **Washington, D.C.**

What is AI?
Imagine computers that can do things—read, write, make complex decisions, and more—that previously required humans. That's artificial intelligence! (AI).

You advise "public sector organizations" on artificial intelligence and finding people to work in AI. Can you tell me what artificial intelligence is? Please tell me about your job.

Artificial intelligence (AI) is the art and science of teaching computers how to "think." If you think about when you use a computer, you have to tell it what to do by pressing the keys or tapping on the screen. But with AI, computers can learn, just like you and me, and they can get better at tasks over time. Some robots can even make their own decisions because they have AI. This means that computers can do a lot more work, and faster.

My job is that I am a consultant—I help organizations and companies find ways to do things better. One of the areas I focus on is helping the federal government use AI to do more work, faster, and at lower cost, so that it can help more people. And to do that, I help them find ways to hire more scientists, engineers, coders, designers, and other technologists who do AI.

What skills are the most important for you to know to do your job?

The most critical skills for my job are problem-solving, listening to my clients, and asking lots of questions. Being able to write and create an argument supported by data is also really important. And I need to be able to present and talk to large groups; I was not always good at this, but I make myself practice a lot!

What do you like best about your job?

My favorite thing about my job is the people I work with and solving really hard problems every day. I love that the work I do can make peoples' lives better, and because I work with the government, that can end up being thousands and thousands of people!

What did you study in college, and where did you go?

I went to the University of Virginia for college (wahoo-wah!) and I studied economics and Spanish. But I was curious, so I also took English, anthropology, music, and history classes. After college, I got a master's in business administration (MBA) from Harvard Business School.

What do you know now that you wish you had known at age ten?

I wish I knew how important it is to find friends that like you just as you are. The world is full of lots of different people—how boring would it be if we were all the same!

What is the one best piece of advice you have for young girls who will be going to high school, college, and joining the workforce in the next decade or so?

Never stop being curious and never stop learning. Learning doesn't just happen in the classroom and it does not end when you get a diploma or a degree. The most successful people I know are always trying new things and are okay with admitting when they don't have the answers. But then they go and find them.

Is there a quote, an inspirational thought, or anything like that that motivates you each day?

"Comparison is the thief of joy."

I used to spend way too much time looking at other people and wishing I was different or could be more like them. I worried I wasn't smart enough or cool enough or pretty enough. Rather than compare myself, now I am happy for other people and their accomplishments, but I don't let them define me or my value.

Can you tell me about a professional or personal setback you had, how you overcame it, and what you learned from it?

My husband got sick a few years after we got married, and it took us years to find out what was causing him to feel tired and bad all the time. For a long time I did not tell my friends or coworkers what was going on because I did not want them to feel bad for me. But when I did finally tell them, the help and support they gave us was amazing. My colleagues helped us find special doctors and they helped me modify my work schedule so that I could do more at home. My friends cooked dinner for us and checked in on me with texts and phone calls and planned movie nights.

My husband is doing much better now, and what I learned is that, even though it is a little bit scary, when we are vulnerable and let people in, a huge weight can be lifted. I thought I was being strong by trying to do everything myself, and what I really needed was to let other people help me.

> **"I thought I was being strong by trying to do everything myself, and what I really needed was to let other people help me."**
>
> —Megan McConnell

Aviation and Aerospace

now

THEN

Julia Cline

Research Aerospace Engineer, NASA Langley Research Center

📍 Langley, Virginia

Maybe you'll set foot on another planet one day!

Hello! You are a Research Aerospace Engineer at NASA Langley Research Center. What does a Research Aerospace Engineer at NASA do?

Aerospace engineers can either work with aircraft or space-craft. I work on the space side. As a research engineer, that means that I investigate challenging problems and determine innovative solutions. At NASA, I do research in two main areas: in-space assembly (ISA) and space nuclear propulsion (SNP). ISA is an exciting research area that encompasses building large structures in space (both on-orbit around planetary bodies and on the surface of other planets). This includes large telescopes (three times bigger than the James Webb Space Telescope!), orbital test bed platforms, and lunar surface construction. I lead a project that investigates using a small robotic crane to offload payloads from a lunar lander that will support our lunar operations.

For SNP, I lead a team looking at a high-temperature materials problem for the nuclear fuel element. The engine must run at very high temperatures (2,700 degrees Celsius) to achieve our goal of transporting humans to Mars with a roundtrip time of about two years. This is a challenge for engineers because there are not a lot of materials that can withstand those temperature ranges. My team is using materials typically used in re-entry heat shields for small tubes in the fuel element to carry hydrogen propellant through the engine. Our work involves computational modeling and experimental testing as well as manufacturing the tubes.

A typical day includes meetings with my team for a few hours—we discuss the current status of the project, challenges that we are experiencing, and come up with a game plan. I may also meet with one of our commercial or academic research partners to discuss their work. I usually have some emails to answer. I'll spend a bit of time working on either a presentation or a paper for our work. Communicating the work we are doing is very important to share with partners and the aerospace community.

What skills are the most important for an aerospace engineer to know?

- A research engineer role must have good engineering skills that come from studying engineering in college.
- Problem solving and critical thinking skills are a must.
- It helps if team members are creative as well—sometimes the best solutions are a bit out of the box.
- Most of the work we do is with a team, so being a good team player and knowing how to work on a team is very important.
- Communication skills are vital! Whether written (like a paper) or verbal (a presentation), being able to tell anyone about the work we are doing is very important. We communicate the scientific advancements in research papers and conference publications, but we also talk to the public through outreach events and media outlets. I need to know how to communicate with a wide variety of audiences and in different communication channels (articles, video, podcasts, etc.). My rule of thumb is that any engineer should be able to explain their work

to their non-engineer family or friends and they should be able to understand!

- Leadership skills are vital. This includes being organized, well-informed, able to make decisions, and empathy for my fellow team members.

What do you like best about being an aerospace engineer?

The people! I work with an amazing group of people at NASA—everyone is passionate about their work and eager to contribute to the success of a project. The people you work with can make a huge difference in how much you enjoy your job. I firmly believe that even if you had your DREAM job, that if the people you worked with suck, you will end up disliking the job.

I also get to work on space topics every single day, and that is pretty dang cool!

What did you study in school, and where did you go?

I studied astrophysics and aerospace engineering (AE) and was in college for a total of eleven years. I received my bachelor's degree in astrophysics from the University of Alberta in 2008, and my master's and PhD in AE from the University of Texas at Arlington in 2011 and 2015, respectively.

What do you know now that you wish you had known at age ten?

You don't have to know exactly what you want to do at the age of ten, or fifteen, or even thirty. Take the time to learn about different areas of study and figure out what you want to do. It is also okay to change your mind and pursue a different path if you decide your original plans aren't for you. The path to how I got to my job at NASA was not a straight line.

Achieving big goals takes a lot of time and effort, but that is okay because you'll get to where you want to be one day. I was about ten when I knew I wanted to be some sort of scientist or engineer. I may have not yet decided that I wanted to work for NASA at that point, but it took me another twenty years to make my dream come true. It's okay that things take time! Keep going!

What is the one best piece of advice you have for young girls who will be going to high school, college, and joining the workforce in the next decade or so?

You belong…. In whatever field you choose, you belong. Don't let anyone tell you differently.

Also, make sure you find yourself a mentor or two. Someone who you admire who is farther ahead of you in the working world that will take the time to talk with you about their career path and give you advice. Don't be afraid to ask someone for advice…. People love to talk about their careers and how they got to where they are!

Is there a quote, an inspirational thought, or anything like that that motivates you each day?

There's a postcard above my desk at NASA that reads, "Dream Big, Focus, and Work Hard," which guides the way I want to show up daily for my job: if I keep doing those three things every day, I know I'll make big things happen. I also think the Arthur Ashe quote "Start where you are. Use what you have. Do what you can" is particularly inspiring, especially when dealing with challenging problems and not knowing where to start!

"Dream Big, Focus, and Work Hard!"

—Julia Cline

now

THEN

Betsy MacLennan

Pilot, First Officer, United Airlines

📍 San Francisco, California

Imagine getting paid to travel the world!

Hello! You are a Boeing 787 pilot for United Airlines. Wow! Tell me about your job.

First of all, I want to say how much I love my job as a pilot. Being a pilot involves many different tasks that may surprise some people. Of course it's always nice to not have to work at a desk in an office. Exploring the world has become my everyday office. I love the physicality of flying, of combining man (or in this case woman) with machine and the fluidity of flight. It can be a wonderful, almost spiritual, experience. However, there are many details involved with the day-to-day operation of working with an airline and getting passengers where they need to go, whether it's on a trip of a lifetime or visiting family and friends. As pilots, we have to stay abreast of the weather conditions, aircraft maintenance issues, federal regulations governing airspace, and rules that keep us safe. It also involves collaboration and good communication with other crew members, refuelers, air traffic controllers, and passengers. So being a pilot is a rich tapestry that involves a variety of skill sets that constantly keep you on your toes!

What skills are the most important for a pilot to know?

Although it's expected that the most important flying skill to become a pilot would be to fly the aircraft accurately and safely, I find there are other skills that are just as critical, if not more important. In my opinion, it's imperative to be a really good communicator to be a safe and effective pilot. Maintaining a flight deck environment where there's open dialogue and a good exchange of ideas helps resolve problems and potentially avoids accidents from occurring. There's constant coordination with the flight attendants and passengers to keep the operation running smoothly.

What do you like best about being a pilot?

What I enjoy most about being a pilot, besides the thrill of actually being able to fly an aircraft most every day, is the lifestyle the job provides. I love being able to travel the world not only while working but on my days off as well. The schedule allows me to typically have at least two weeks off a month to spend time with my family or pursue other interests as well as travel with the flight benefits provided by the airline, which is one of many perks of working in the travel industry.

What did you study in college, and where did you go?

I attended the University of Southern California in Los Angeles, California, and studied international relations. Although at the time I was interested in pursuing law school, I was always interested in travel and learning to speak several languages. I think the love of travel led me to explore pursuing the field of aviation. It's not a requirement to get a degree in aeronautical engineering or aviation, however, getting a bachelor's degree is important if you want to pursue a career as a pilot.

What do you know now that you didn't know when you were nine, ten, or eleven?

What I know now that I wished I had known at ten years of age is that I could dream bigger and bolder than I realized. The sky's the limit. There is nothing you can't do if you dream it. You can truly reach the stars if you want to!

What is the one best piece of advice you have for young girls who will be going to high school, college, and entering the workforce in the next decade or so?

My one piece of advice to young girls moving forward with their education is to always lead with curiosity and keep their options open. Push the envelope and explore learning about different fields of interest that challenge you to think and learn differently. Do things that push you out of your comfort zone so you can challenge yourself and grow academically and as a person.

Is there a quote, an inspirational thought, or anything like that that motivates you?

Every day I do a gratitude journal that puts me in a proper mindset to accomplish all of the goals I set for myself. Having a positive attitude and outlook on life gives me the freedom to live a purposeful and joyful life.

> **"Push the envelope and explore learning about different fields of interest that challenge you to think and learn differently."**
>
> —Betsy MacLennan

Biotechnology and Pharmaceutical

now

THEN

Pam Randhawa

 Chief Executive Officer, Emperiko Corp.

📍 Cambridge, Massachusetts

New drugs to fight terrible diseases!

Hello! You are the chief executive officer at Empiriko. What is Empiriko? Tell me about your job.

Empiriko is a biotech company that has developed a novel *in vitro* biomimetic platform (liver-on-a-chip) to accelerate its small molecule drug development with a current focus on antiviral therapies for HIV/AIDS. The company is also developing a point-of-care diagnostic platform for personalized immunologic/genetic biomarker and drug monitoring. The data flow between these platforms enables Empiriko to cost-effectively accelerate drug development and customize patient treatment for improved clinical outcomes.

The CEO develops company strategy, direction, and manages overall operations. This includes delegating and directing projects, driving growth and profitability, managing organizational structure, and communicating with employees, partners, the board of directors, investors, and other stakeholders. Since we are a startup, I take on added responsibilities of negotiating partnerships and investment deals that may typically be done by finance and business development executives.

What skills are the most important for you to know to do your job?

One of the biggest challenges for any company is to find the right employees to ensure success. Every CEO and executive needs critical skills to identify the right talent and to attract and retain them for a long time.

When I started Empiriko, I had to assemble the right team who could execute on our vision. Aside from building the internal team, attracting partners, advisors, and experts is one of the most important drivers of success in the startup and business world. When more formidable people are happy to help us, I know that we substantially increase our chances of success. The art of selling and convincing investors, partners, board of directors, advisors, and employees on the company's vision is one of the key skills that every CEO should have no matter the stage of their company.

At the earlier stages of the company, founders and their teams make mistakes and pivot ideas frequently. More established companies sometimes lose market share because they did not keep up with innovation and market needs. A CEO must have a clear understanding of how to create value through innovation for both shareholders and stakeholders. I continue to explore out-of-the-box ideas and identify trends, threats, and opportunities that others may not see. To select the right ideas/strategy and effectively execute on those ideas requires a team-oriented approach, but I also believe in independent thinking to solve problems. My analytical mind and math skills enable me to collect and analyze relevant information from external sources to make decisions based on facts. We are a science-based company, and making decisions based on data is critical. My parents were avid readers and believed in lifelong learning. They instilled this practice in me and my siblings. Each day, I spend three to four hours reading clinical studies and industry-related news. This helps me discuss complex topics with chemists, biologists, physicians, engineers, and business professionals to develop strategy, make decisions, and solve problems. In addition, this helps me to be a more effective communicator with internal team members and external stakeholders—an important skill required for a CEO.

What do you like best about your job?

I love working with brilliant scientists, engineers, and business experts to create disruptive technologies that could help improve and save millions of lives.

What did you study in college, and where did you go?

I earned my undergraduate degree from the University of Rajasthan in Jaipur, India, majoring in economics, political science, and English literature. My master's degree from Carnegie Mellon was in public management with a focus on healthcare.

What do you know now that you wish you had known at age ten?

I was born and raised in India, and I was fortunate to have an idyllic childhood. Both my parents valued free thinking, education, hard work, and doing things that were not normal or traditional. During those days, Indian parents typically pressured their kids to study and not to participate in extracurricular activities. However, my parents believed in learning and experiencing things beyond the academic curriculum. I was allowed to play sports at a very young age (seven years old), and I even traveled to other cities to compete in one-hundred-and two hundred-meter races with my coaches and other athletes. I continued with sports and other activities throughout high school and college. I lived in the moment and enjoyed every aspect of my life.

My mother was an entrepreneur who leased agricultural land and then contracted it out for farming. This allowed her to have lots of free time to spend with me and my three older brothers. When I was seven years old, I attended several of her negotiation meetings. As the only woman in the room with tough landowners, she commanded respect. She was a fair but shrewd negotiator. To this day, when I am working on a deal, I remind myself how my mother conducted those meetings. Looking back, I think that she pioneered Take Your Daughter to Work Day.

What I know today about my mom's fearless and bold approach to personal and professional life, I wish I knew at age ten to ask her more questions and thank her more often.

What is the one best piece of advice you have for young girls who will be going to high school, college, and joining the workforce in the next decade or so?

Never be afraid to be different than anyone else and ask for help when necessary, but know that there is no replacement for hard work. Don't let negative people live rent-free in your head and don't underestimate the power of positive energy, charisma, and optimism.

Can you tell me about a professional or personal setback you had, how you overcame it, and what you learned from it?

When I was seventeen, my mother suddenly passed away from a stroke. She was forty-eight years old. It was a tragic and transformative experience that changed my life forever. I never fully got over the trauma, but with time and lots of love from family and friends, I learned how to make a way to live with it easier. I wanted to honor her memory in a way that was meaningful for me and represented who she was as a woman. I started dreaming about developing a solution to help others in a similar health situation and learn to identify early symptoms of heart disease.

I did not study medicine or science during my undergraduate years because I intended to be an economist. However, my family moved to the U.S. in the late eighties, and I thought it was a fresh start for me to learn about the healthcare industry. I took a clerical job at a local teaching hospital in Boston before going to graduate school full-time. With this first introduction to the healthcare and medical industry, I decided to become an entrepreneur in this space.

After graduate study in public management focusing on healthcare and policy, I worked in various segments of the healthcare and life sciences industry for fifteen-plus years to gain knowledge and experience. I admit that this was my calculated strategy to be prepared enough to start a company that I dreamed about after my mother's passing to keep her memory alive and help others who may be suffering from the condition that took her life. Since starting the company, our focus has been to develop a platform and applications for personalizing diagnostics and treatment for patients suffering from cardiovascular diseases. We are now closer to having a product that we think will transform medicine and clinical decision-making. This was a major learning experience in so many ways that you can not only turn tragic events into opportunities to do good, but also you can achieve anything you desire if you continue to stay focused and work hard.

Is there a quote, an inspirational thought, or anything like that that motivates you each day?

> *"Do not go where the path may lead, go instead where there is no path and leave a trail." —Ralph Waldo Emerson*

Julia Taylor Brandus

Is there anything you would like to add that we are not asking here?

I am a minority immigrant woman but I never felt at a disadvantage. In the United States, hard work, expertise, and intellect are respected. With hard work and tenacity, I captured opportunities and flourished.

> "There is no replacement for hard work. Don't let negative people live rent-free in your head and don't underestimate the power of positive energy, charisma, and optimism."
>
> —Pam Randhawa

Blockchain, Crypto, and Digital Currencies

Amy Kim

 Policy Lead for Blockchain, Crypto, and Digital Currencies, PayPal Inc.

📍 **Washington, D.C.**

Cash is so yesterday. These days, money exists in electronic form!

Hello! You are the Policy Lead for Blockchain, Crypto, and Digital Currencies at PayPal. Tell me about PayPal, blockchain, and digital currencies.

PayPal is a payment services provider that has one central mission: to democratize financial services to ensure that everyone, regardless of background or economic standing, has access to affordable, convenient, and secure products and services to take control of their financial lives. With respect to crypto, PayPal now enables customers the opportunity to buy, sell, hold, transfer, and check out with several crypto currencies, including bitcoin, ether, litecoin, and bitcoin cash.

My role is to assess the policy and legal landscape surrounding crypto and engage with government officials to ensure they understand the technology and PayPal's products and vision within that landscape. I talk to government officials and experts in industry and academia to stay on top of developing trends and share our perspectives on the future of this technology. Often this includes our views on how policy objectives can be met through legislation.

What skills are the most important for someone in your role to know?

Having a strong background in a key area impacting this space is important. For me, that's anti-money laundering and counter-terrorism finance laws and regulations. Because crypto involves the transfer of value, digitally, it triggers concerns that bad actors could also try to use it. Having this skill in a traditional area of law really helped launch me into this space early on, and continues to be an area that I enjoy tackling policy objectives and finding ways to match the beneficial aspects of this technology.

Over the last five years I've been able to expand that expertise into understanding the policy and legal challenges in a number of areas impacting crypto, and I've found that another essential skill is the ability to see the law as it exists today, understand whether or not it will achieve its underlying objectives when applied to crypto, and, if not, what changes are needed to achieve them. That flexibility in mindset and the ability to look ahead and think about positive change is also an important skill in this evolving industry.

What do you like best about your job?

I love being a part of a community that is striving to enable technology that will make people's financial lives work more efficiently and effectively. It is really an extraordinary group of people who are driven to achieve their goals and have been some of the most inspirational people I have met. It's a wonderful network.

What did you study in school, and where did you go?

I was an international relations major with a political science minor at Pepperdine University. After that I received my JD from the University of Notre Dame. I always knew I wanted to travel and work with people of different backgrounds. While crypto wasn't around when I first graduated, it enabled me to tie in my international compliance work with the development of a new and exciting industry that crosses borders.

What do you know now that you wish you had known at age ten?

Actually, I kind of knew then not to worry about what other people think. I was much better at knowing it than following it, but you definitely need to follow what's in your gut and in your heart. If you like school, then own that and dive in. Don't worry about the fact that some of the cooler kids seem to be casual about it. If you're great at building Minecraft cities, then go for it (while still working hard at school!). I find it relevant even today; people point out to me that the price of bitcoin is down, the market is down, the industry is tanking. I know that this technology is more than the price of one token. The underlying fundamentals of it will be transformative and you have to keep your eyes forward. The key is to have a goal (or two or three), which will help you stay focused and make choices that lead you in the right direction.

What is the one best piece of advice you have for young girls who will be going to high school, college, and joining the workforce in the next decade or so?

This is a tough one. On the one hand, I believe that girls have excellent tools and education around them to be able to succeed if they are driven to do it (whatever success is to them). On the other, it's always surprising to find that, even today, it's possible to run into mindsets that are not sensitive to the backgrounds of different people. I find the best way to maneuver through that is to imagine success, visualize achieving that goal, that position, that idea, and keep working toward it. Don't let people say it won't work, or it's not the right time, or you may not be ready. Keep striving for that goal. And remember your own value—you bring a lot of skills and background and perspective to what you do. Remember that it is valuable!

Is there a quote, an inspirational thought, or anything like that that motivates you each day?

My kids! I hope that I am a good role model for them—in the little everyday things and the bigger things that take more time to accomplish. I also know that I need to keep working on my own challenges and constantly strive to be a little bit better. If I continue to learn and grow, they will too.

> "Don't let people say it won't work, or it's not the right time, or you may not be ready. Keep striving for that goal."
>
> —Amy Kim

Cybersecurity

now

THEN

Leslie Anderson

Chief Strategist, Cybersecurity Operations, MITRE Corp.

📍 Arlington, Virginia

All kinds of information—including about you—is online. Cybersecurity helps protect it.

Hello! You are the Chief Strategist for Cybersecurity Operations at MITRE Corp. What is MITRE Corp., and what is a cybersecurity strategist?

MITRE is a nonprofit organization that operates federally funded research and development centers for the federal government. Our mission is solving problems for a safer world. Our government sponsors include a wide range of defense and civilian agencies. My job is to work with MITRE cybersecurity teams as well as our government sponsors to define strategies, develop new capabilities, and manage special projects—all aimed at protecting and defending cyberspace.

What skills are the most important for you to know?

I've found the most valuable skills to be an excellent communicator and quick learner. It is certainly important to know about cybersecurity because that is the focus of my work, but it hasn't always been the focus. Maintaining excellent communications is critical to creating high-performing teams, no matter the purpose of the work.

What do you like best about your role?

Every day I feel like I'm working on projects and with people who make the world a safer place. That makes it easy to get out of bed in the morning! And in the end, it's always been the talented people with whom I work that make it worth it.

What did you study in school, and where did you go?

My undergrad degree is from Carnegie Mellon, where I earned a dual bachelor's in professional writing and German. It was the first time I was truly surrounded by technologists and scientists, which has become a standing theme in my professional life! My graduate degree is a master of fine arts in creative writing from Columbia University.

What do you know now that you wish you had known at age ten?

I know now that I'm capable of doing most things I set my mind to. When I was ten, I believed I wasn't good at math and science because they were harder subjects for me. So, even though I found science very interesting, I didn't pursue it. If I'd had more confidence and better coaching, I probably would have explored a different educational path.

What is the one best piece of advice you have for young girls who will be going to high school, college, and joining the workforce in the next decade or so?

Keep an open mind about opportunities as they present themselves. Say "yes" as much as you can to learning and trying new things. And when you are interested in something, show it; being genuinely interested in what you are doing is a critical ingredient in the recipe for success.

> **"Say 'yes' as much as you can to learning and trying new things."**
>
> —Leslie Anderson

Data Science

Janet Jones-Oliveira

Data Scientist and Director of Advanced Technology, Verite Group, Inc.

Sterling, Virginia

Analyzing numbers—data—helps individuals, businesses, and governments make better decisions.

You are the Director of Advanced Technology at Verite Group. Wow! What do you do? Please tell me about your job. You are also a data scientist! Please tell me about that!

I solve problems for a living—and I love it! I have been very fortunate to have had the privilege and responsibility to work on some of the toughest problems facing our country. The first thing that I do is to listen to the person who has the problem. Then I answer "Janet's five questions." If the answer to *all* five questions is yes, then there is a high likelihood that our proposal will result in a contract to provide an answer to the sponsor. Here are the questions:

- Do they have a problem?
- Do they own the problem?
- Do they want an answer to the problem?
- Do they have the money to solve the problem?
- Do they want us to give them the solution?

What skills are the most important for you to know to be a data scientist?

First and foremost, one needs to be a scientist. A scientist is a person who is a subject-area expert in one, or preferably more, of the natural or physical sciences. In particular, a data scientist must also like numbers enough to study what the numbers actually mean. A data scientist must build a model of the problem, taking into account all of the relevant factors, and then solve the problem. He or she must then make an assessment of the solution by doing what is called "V&V," or "Validation & Verification."

Validation is the process of checking whether the specification of the model captures the customer's requirements, while verification is the process of checking that the computer software meets the specification.

In other words, you must assess whether you are computing the right thing and is the calculation being done correctly. It is your responsibility to get the right answer to the right problem.

What do you like best about your job?

I have never been bored because I have never been asked to solve the same problem twice. Every new problem posed has presented a new opportunity to learn more about our world.

What did you study in college, and where did you go?

I went to college for a very long time because I enjoyed the academic life—it was fun, and I was not in a hurry to go and make money. I was very fortunate to be able to continue my education with relatively little school debt because graduate school in STEM (Science, Technology, Engineering, and Mathematics) usually comes with a teaching or research assistantship, which covers tuition and living expenses!

I earned a bachelor of arts from Smith College in mathematics, with minors in art and sociology—my senior project was in operations research. I graduated from the University of Pennsylvania with a master of architecture—for my thesis, I designed a space station. I then went to work for an engineering company that designed energy-efficiency corrective measures for buildings.

I then attended the Massachusetts Institute of Technology (MIT) and earned a master's in aeronautics and astronautics; for my thesis, I solved a fluid-solid interaction engineering problem.

I won an international graduate competition in Aero/Astro engineering for my space station design in architecture!

Finally, I earned an interdepartmental Doctor of Philosophy (PhD) from MIT in mathematical physics.

I do not hold any two degrees in the same subject.

Then, I went off to learn so much more working for the Department of Energy at two of our National Laboratories.

I have designed engineering solutions on the ground, under the ground, on the water, under the water, in air, in space, and I have worked in plasma physics. I love science and I love data.

What do you know now that you wish you had known at age ten?

This is a tough question for me—my parents divorced when I was about your age. I wish that I knew that I had already learned everything that I needed from my parents. Yes, there was still all of life to live and learn, but the foundational values and the ethics that they had taught me were already established in my being by age ten. You are who you will become, and you are beautiful.

What is the one best piece of advice you have for young girls who will be going to high school, college, and joining the workforce in the next decade or so?

Find someone who loves math and science, who is able to share the excitement that they have for their work with you. Call me!

Can you tell me about a professional or personal setback you had, how you overcame it, and what you learned from it?

I have had my work plagiarized numerous times.* I do not know if this happens to women more often than to men or not, but your response to it is critical. Brush your feelings off and keep going.

Is there a quote, an inspirational thought, or anything like that that motivates you each day?

The golden rule: "Do unto others as you would have them do unto you."

Is there anything you would like to add that we are not asking here?

I want you to know that with the love and support of your family and friends and community, there is nothing that you cannot do.

I returned to work full-time when our son was six weeks old, and again when our daughter was seven weeks old (once there was an opening for her at our daycare center). You can do it all, when you learn to ask for and receive and provide help to and from others—make plans.

---

* Plagiarism is when someone takes the work you have done and pretends like they did that work. They present it as their own and take credit for it. It is very unethical and dishonest. It is akin to cheating and lying.

"I want you to know that with the love and support of your family and friends and community, there is nothing that you cannot do."

—Janet Jones-Oliveira

Economics, Finance, and Venture Capital

now

THEN

Marguerita Cheng, CFP

Chief Executive Officer, Blue Ocean Global Wealth

📍 Gaithersburg, Maryland

Financial advisors help people manage their money—save, invest, and make more!

Hello! You are the CEO of Blue Ocean Global Wealth, an investment advisory firm. What is an investment advisory firm, and what do you do?

Blue Ocean Global Wealth is a financial planning and investment advisory firm. Our mission is to provide families, financial advisors, corporations, and institutions with prudent financial advice, including risk management and investment knowledge. We embrace global diversity and steward the protection, growth, and distribution of our clients' wealth.

In order to do your job, what skills are the most important for you to know?

I think listening is probably one of the most important skills. Because I'm both right- and left-brained, I can readily adapt to our clients' needs. By helping clients focus on their life financial goals, they feel less overwhelmed and stressed. For more detail-oriented clients, I can make the complex less confusing, but I have to pull them out of the weeds first and focus them on the big picture. Early in my career, I had managers tell me that I wasn't aggressive enough to be a financial advisor. For sure, the financial planner of the future must deliver results with confidence, empathy, and emotional intelligence!

What do you like best about being a financial planner?

Financial planning is intellectually stimulating and emotionally gratifying. I value the meaningful long-term relationships we have with our clients. It is so rewarding to experience the positive impact we have on our clients' lives.

Julia Taylor Brandus

What did you study in college, and where did you go?

I earned a BS in finance and a BA in East Asian language and literature at the University of Maryland in College Park. As the recipient of the Monbukagakusho Scholarship, a prestigious academic scholarship offered by the Japanese government, I also had the opportunity to study at Keio University in Tokyo, Japan.

What do you know now that you wish you had known at age ten?

Knowing what you like is very important. It is also important to challenge yourself and try new things without fear of failure or judgment. I'm the eldest of three girls. I knew how important it was to be a good role model for my immediate family, my extended family, and my community. I am the first one to attend college on my mom's side of the family. At age ten, I lived in the Netherlands with my family. I enjoyed meeting new people and visiting new places. I may have not felt comfortable speaking up and speaking out. I think it's important for girls to express themselves.

What is the one best piece of advice you have for young girls who will be going to high school, college, and joining the workforce in the next decade or so?

I think mentors can be very helpful. Sometimes, I may have been uncomfortable asking for help. Asking for help is not a sign of weakness. It demonstrates courage and commitment to self-improvement and lifelong learning.

Is there a quote, an inspirational thought, or anything like that that motivates you each day?

Don't be intimidated by what you don't know. That can be your greatest strength and ensure that you do things differently from everyone else.

> "Asking for help is not a sign of weakness. It demonstrates courage and commitment to self-improvement and life-long learning."
>
> —Marguerita Cheng

Schelo Doirin

 Founder,
Black Women Invest

📍 **Dallas, Texas**

The mission: providing Women of Color with the tools and support to invest in both the stock market and the real estate market.

Hello! You're the founder of Black Women Invest. What is that, and what do you do?

When I founded Black Women Invest in 2019, my intention was to provide Women of Color with a "safe space" to speak about money. After realizing that many of the women who joined my online community were not equipped with the basic knowledge needed to live comfortably or prepare for retirement, I decided to turn Black Women Invest into a business. In addition to cultivating an online community through Facebook, I now provide women with educational resources focusing on investing. I created an academy, designed to give women the confidence to invest in both the stock market and the real estate market, despite their income.

What skills are the most important for you to know to do your job?

- Investment knowledge
- The ability to educate and empower others

Influencing someone to do something they aren't used to is a skill that is essential for my role. The reason is because if I provide someone with the knowledge on how to invest, it doesn't mean they will actually open an investment account or buy the property that will make them money. The best leaders are those who can influence and empower others around them to take action. Since I want the women in my community to apply the knowledge they're learning, influencing AND communication are essential skills that I continuously sharpen.

What do you like best about your job?

I enjoy being a part of the "aha" moments that my clients and community members receive when they finally understand a concept or a term that they didn't understand before.

I also thoroughly enjoy seeing the women share their financial "wins." Whether they are buying an investment property or opening a retirement account for the first time ever, witnessing the joy they experience is priceless.

The next best part is the freedom I have through owning and running my own business.

Owning my own business also means that I have the freedom to make as much money as I desire. Typically, when you work for someone, the salary the employer provides is the limit for your income. This is not the case when you have your own business! My salary, my impact, and my legacy are in my own hands.

What did you study in college, and where did you go?

I studied finance at Florida International University. I also found an interest in African studies and marketing, and took many courses in both of those subjects as well.

What do you know now that you wish you had known at age ten?

One of the most important lessons life has taught me is that you lose 100 percent of the shots you don't take. When I was ten, I was very excited about life and I had dreams to do many things. As I got older, I allowed fear to stop me from ever even trying most of those dreams out.

I wish I knew that it doesn't matter what the outcome of those shots would've been. By believing in myself enough to take every opportunity, I would establish a stronger intuition and a deeper confidence in my own abilities a lot sooner in life.

What is the one best piece of advice you have for young girls who will be going to high school, college, and joining the workforce in the next decade or so?

Travel the world. The world you know is small. You have your parents, your neighborhood, your friends, your classmates. You probably go to the same grocery store every week, attend the same church every weekend, ride your bike down the same path every day, etc. And today, this may appear to be a big world. But it's not, there's more out there.

When you go to high school and college, be open to learning about other people and other cultures. Seek opportunities to volunteer abroad, study abroad, work or intern abroad. What you will quickly learn is that most of the world doesn't live like you do. Experiencing this will contribute to you finding your calling in life. It will stretch your mind to think of creative solutions to the problems you see.

Is there a quote, an inspirational thought, or anything like that that motivates you each day?

There is a song that has motivated me for the last ten-plus years. It is actually my favorite song of all time: "I Hope You Dance" by Lee Ann Womack. Every line in this song is a powerful reminder of the importance of "dancing" or taking advantage of every opportunity presented to you. It speaks of the short time we are given on this earth and that in every element of our lives (spiritually, physically, mentally, emotionally, etc.), we should take chances, never settle, love others, be forgiving, never give up, and have faith in ourselves and in God.

"The best leaders are those who can influence and empower others around them to take action."

—Schelo Doirin

now

THEN

Constance Hunter

Economist, Executive Vice President, Global Head of Strategy and ESG (Environmental, Social, and Governance), American International Group, Inc. (AIG)

📍 New York, New York

Economists study money, labor, and other resources and how they are used by people, companies, and governments!

Hi! You are an economist and executive vice president, global head of strategy and ESG for AIG. What is AIG? What is ESG? And what do you do?

I'm an economist. I draw upon that, plus my experience as an investor and leader, to try and analyze and anticipate market and economic trends and determine how AIG—which is a finance and insurance company—can capitalize on them. ESG stands for Environmental, Social, and Governance. We think that the transition to a cleaner energy future will be a challenging one, but that economists, energy experts, and scientists, partnering with our stakeholders, can develop sustainable, effective, and profitable solutions.

What skills are the most important for a chief economist to know? I'll bet math is really important!

Well, so I would say math is really important to know, but I would say one of the biggest skills is empathy. Because if you don't understand who your audience is, and you don't understand who you're communicating to and what their vantage point is, you can do all the math in the world. But if you can't communicate that math to another person, and you can't understand where they're coming from, then you probably aren't gonna make it to be the chief economist. You might be an economist somewhere, but you're not gonna make it to be the chief economist! So math and empathy are the two big things.

What do you like best about being an economist?

What I like best is that I've met and become friends with so many other economists, and we all have a passion for figuring out the economy, which is really like a big jigsaw puzzle. But one thing that's different is that we don't have a picture on the front of the box. We just have all the pieces and we have to figure it out without the picture. So we're always asking, "How do all those pieces fit together?" And sometimes that's really hard. So it's great to have other economists who have the same training as you do. And to talk about what's happening and to come up with ideas and to work together on research projects. And so my favorite thing about being an economist is solving these economic puzzles with all these amazing friends.

What did you study in college, and where did you go?

I went to New York University and studied economics. But I also studied sociology, which is the study of groups of people. That's different from psychology, which is the study of individuals. Sociology is sort of a form of psychology. It's how do people in society behave? How do groups behave? And it turned out that combining this with economics was really valuable because after I went to college, a whole new field of economics was invented called behavioral economics. It was invented because all the mathematicians realized that their models of how people should behave didn't always line up with how people *actually* behaved. And then I went to graduate school and I got a master's degree at Columbia University, which was really great. And I studied with a lot of amazing, really smart professors. And I have many really, really good friends from when I was in graduate school.

I also wanted to add this other thing which is really important. I belong to an organization called the National Association for Business Economics (it's called NABE for short). It has a lot of continuing education classes that are just terrific. This is important because if you want to stay at the top of your profession, you have to keep on learning. So even after you graduate with a college degree or even two degrees, you have to keep taking classes and keep learning and keep refreshing your skills so that you stay relevant. And that's how you stay at the top of your game.

What do you know now that you didn't know when you were nine, ten, or eleven?

Oh, whew. That's a tough one. Probably a lot of things! But I'll tell you what the beautiful thing about being that age is. You have a lot of freedom to think about new things and be creative and use your imagination. What I wish I knew is that when you get to be an adult, if you do it right, you'll be able to do so many of the things that you love to do, even when you're eleven. So I know you like to rock climb and you like dogs. You can have a good career and still do those things! You never have to stop doing the things that make you happy!

What is the one best piece of advice you have for young girls who will be going to high school, college, and entering the workforce in the next decade or so?

My best piece of advice is figure out something that you really care about. Something that really interests you. Something that you can't stop thinking about. And then figure out how to do that with discipline and energy.

Is there a quote, an inspirational thought, or anything like that which motivates you?

Yes. I have a motto, which is that you can't worry about things you can't control. Time is valuable! Don't waste it worrying about things you can't control.

"Time is valuable! Don't waste it worrying about things you can't control."

—Constance Hunter

now

THEN

Esther Lee

 Chief Executive Officer, Refraction (technology innovation hub)

◉ McLean, Virginia

Want to start a company one day?

Hello! You are the CEO of Refraction. What is Refraction, and what do you do?

Refraction is a nonprofit innovation hub that provides mentoring, programs, and office space for startups and entrepreneurs. Our mission is to help startups in technology and other fields grow and create jobs here in the greater Washington, D.C. region. A CEO (chief executive officer) leads a company or organization, overseeing all aspects of the company or organization, including strategy, sales, marketing, and operations.

What skills are the most important for someone in your role to know?

A great CEO needs many skills, but for my role at Refraction, the most important skills are networking (to connect entrepreneurs to key mentors, investors, and partners), partnership (to create impactful partnerships), and fundraising (to raise money for the nonprofit).

What do you like best about your role?

I love my job because I have the opportunity to work closely with great entrepreneurs (who are building amazing companies), mentors (who want to give back by helping entrepreneurs), and partners (who invest their time and money in Refraction because they believe in our mission).

What did you study in college, and where did you go?

I studied economics at Harvard University and earned an MBA (master of business administration) at the MIT Sloan School of Management.

What do you know now that you wish you had known at age ten?

I wish I knew at age ten how important strong relationships and teamwork are in work and life. No one person, no matter how smart or successful he or she may be, can accomplish what a great team can do together.

What is the one best piece of advice you have for young girls who will be going to high school, college, and joining the workforce in the next decade or so?

You can do anything you want with hard work and great mentors. Dream big and pursue your passion!

Is there a quote, an inspirational thought, or anything like that that motivates you each day?

"Genius is one percent inspiration and ninety-nine percent perspiration," by Thomas Edison, who invented the light bulb, movie camera, and record player. This is inspiring because it reminds me that we can do anything if we work hard.

> "No one person, no matter how smart or successful he or she may be, can accomplish what a great team can do together."
>
> —Esther Lee

now

THEN

Kimberly Smith Spacek

 Head of Capital Formation, TechStars

📍 New York, New York

How to get money to start a company!

Hello! You are a venture capitalist. Please tell me about your job.

Venture capital is very exciting to me because it is really the engine of the economy. We help create new businesses. Say you have an idea. We'll work with you to form that idea, create a prototype, a business plan, help you execute it, and then bring you out to the world. Venture capital firms are part of that journey. So we make investments in your company at the earliest stages. And hopefully along the way, help you grow your business. Over time, as you continue to perform well, you make money, you hire people. Then you really start to have what we call revenue, which is profit and losses coming in because you have a lot of expenses, right?

As you hire employees and give them healthcare and infrastructure, like setting up office space and buying computers, you have to spend money. But as your business grows and you create revenue, more people get interested in it. And so it starts out with venture capital, and then over time, your company may kind of graduate to other types of investments, whether it's private equity and then into the public markets, meaning the stock market!

But before all that glitz and glamor and standing at the New York Stock Exchange and ringing the bell (to open or close that day's trading session), it starts with an idea. And so venture capital is kind of the engine that helps create all this, it helps it all come together.

What skills are most important for a venture capitalist?

Knowledge is key. Really knowing your business, knowing your audience, is probably first and foremost. And so before I meet with an investor, I make sure I do a little research on them. I create a little dossier, everything I can find on the internet about the person I'm going to meet. Building relationships is important, but that all starts with knowing your audience. And a large portion of that is listening. I always say to my children and to people, the best advice I got for my father was listen to learn.

What do you like best about being a venture capitalist?

Meeting new people. I love talking to people. I love hearing about their stories. I also love helping entrepreneurs. It is so amazing being around people with their ideas at the earliest stage. And they're trying to figure things out. They're willing to take risks on things that no one's done before that to many people seem insane. Like, this is the craziest idea. But, being around people that have these crazy, creative ideas that will sacrifice everything to execute them—it's so rewarding. It's so invigorating. And it really makes me excited to work in venture capital to continue to meet these people and hear all these new ideas all the time. But that is my favorite part. Just being around these entrepreneurs, building relationships with new people, new companies every day. It makes me excited to get out of bed every morning.

What did you study in school?

I went to a small liberal arts college called Middlebury College in Vermont. My primary discipline was political science, and I minored in Spanish and in biology.

What do you know now that you wish you had known at age ten?

Not to doubt myself as much. And to trust my gut. I wish I had trusted my gut earlier. Sometimes I let the inner demon in me push me in the wrong direction. It was really a lack of confidence in myself.

I'll add that sometimes girls need a little more. When I see a fiery girl, I'm proud of them because I think you have to push forward, and that's how you get the big jobs, by taking risks. So confidence is definitely okay.

What is the one best piece of advice you have for young girls who will be going to high school, college, and joining the workforce soon?

It's important to listen to others. But you also have a voice. You have to make sure that you have confidence in yourself so that you feel comfortable having a voice in the room. And I think that is really the key to being a successful woman in the workplace. A lot of times I would work the longest, and I'm not afraid of hard work and I'm proud of it. But when I think about it now, I think that reflected the fact that I lacked confidence in myself. So I think having confidence in yourself at a young age is very important.

Is there a cool or an inspirational thought or anything like that that motivates you each day?

It's very corny, but it takes zero effort to be nice to people. To share a smile with someone. Before I hire someone I take them out to lunch, and one of the things I judge them by is how they treat the wait staff at the restaurants. If they're not kind to them—and they could be the most qualified people by far—I won't hire them. So I always tell myself and my children it takes zero effort to be nice.

Can you tell me about a professional or personal setback you had and how you overcame it and what you learned from it?

I had a big professional setback last year. I was up for a corporate board seat. And at the time I was a partner at a $16 billion hedge fund. I was one of the only female partners, and I was trashed in the newspaper as being unqualified. One of the things I do on the side is raise awareness for mental health issues that plague our veterans. And instead of talking about my twenty-five-year career on Wall Street, my undergrad degree from one of the top colleges in the country, my MBA, they said I run a small apparel business and that I was completely unqualified for the role. And this was splashed all over the financial press, and I didn't get the seat.

But this turned out to be a blessing, because you don't want to work with bad people, and they were bad people. And they were obviously going out of their way to disparage me, but it hurt because I was qualified for the role. It was at a wealth advisory firm. There was no one on the slate, quite frankly, that had more experience than me in that sector. While I didn't have public board experience, I had plenty of nonprofit board experience and I had plenty of experience in what they were trying to do. And I did cry. I was shattered by how they disparaged me in the media, how I was treated, and ultimately didn't get the job. And what I learned from it after going through all the ups and downs, I didn't want to be with bad people. It goes back to what I said: it takes zero effort to be nice to people. There are ways that they could have talked about me, but they took a nasty route. So it was a blessing because I wouldn't have to spend time with bad people.

Is there anything you would like to add that we're not asking here?

I want to really say don't be afraid to take a risk. Do things that push you, particularly when you're young. Push your boundaries a little bit, as long as you don't get in trouble or do anything illegal, but push yourself because if you don't, you'll regret it later and you don't want to live a life of regret. Pursue things, take risks, even if—and particularly if—they're hard. Rewards come with risk.

> **"Push yourself because if you don't, you'll regret it later and you don't want to live a life of regret."**
>
> —Kimberly Smith Spacek

Education

now

THEN

Ruth Ben-Ghiat

Professor, New York University; Historian, Author, and Commentator

📍 New York, New York

Studying the past can help us understand the present— and the future.

Among other things, you are a professor of history at New York University (maybe I should go there in a few years!). Please tell me about your jobs.

I teach undergraduates' and graduate students' classes about fascism, World War Two, Italy, war and cinema, propaganda, and authoritarianism. It is very gratifying to teach and help people learn to think and write better.

I also have another job doing media commentary for television, radio, and print journalism, and I write op-eds for MSNBC, CNN, and other places about politics.

And I publish a newsletter, *Lucid*, about threats to democracy. I write essays, interview people, and hold live Q&As.

It's a busy life but very fulfilling.

What skills are the most important for you to know to do your jobs?

My job is about communication, oral and written. If you can't explain things clearly, you'll never be a good teacher. I also have to be a clear and engaging writer and commentator. Luckily, I love writing, so that part of things comes naturally.

For television you also need to be poised and calm.

What do you like best about your jobs?

Interacting with students and readers and helping people to understand what we are living through and what happened in the past—why that matters for today.

What did you study in college, and where did you go?

I wanted to be a lawyer, so I started out studying political science. Then I worked for a law firm part-time, and decided law was not for me. So I switched to a history major, and that's what I ended up doing. I went to UCLA (University of

California, Los Angeles) and lived at home. My immigrant father did not think I should go away to college. Luckily I loved UCLA.

What do you know now that you wish you had known at age ten?

That parents love you in their own way even though they may seem distant. That people can be unkind, like people at school, because they are insecure. And there are plenty of people who want to help if you know how to reach out to them.

What is the one best piece of advice you have for young girls who will be going to high school, college, and joining the workforce in the next decade or so?

Believe in yourself and have confidence in your own abilities. Trust your instincts and take time to sit with yourself and listen to what your heart is telling you.

Is there a quote, an inspirational thought, or anything like that that motivates you each day?

That each day is a gift.

Can you tell me about a professional or personal setback you had, how you overcame it, and what you learned from it?

Academics is full of setbacks—no one wants to publish your book, no one accepts your articles, you apply for grants and get none of them. The key to overcoming setbacks is trying again, having tenacity. Many people only talk about their successes, and so we don't realize that almost everyone who has a prestigious fellowship applied to many others they did not get. I try to be transparent about all the professional rejections I have had so that others don't fall into this trap.

"The key to overcoming setbacks is trying again, having tenacity."

—Ruth Ben-Ghiat

now

THEN

Gail Helt

Assistant Professor of Political Science, Director of the King Security and Intelligence Studies, King University; former Central Intelligence Agency officer (working on issues related to East Asian security, politics, and governance)

📍 **Bristol, Tennessee**

Political science is the study of politics, our government, and the people who run it.

Hello! You spent many years at the CIA. What is the CIA, and what did you do?

The CIA provides the president and other high-level policy-makers with analysis on everything going on in the world that might impact American interests, so they can take action to prevent harm to the United States or our allies. This includes things like the activities of terrorist groups, any actions our enemies are taking, and even climate change! The CIA also recruits spies throughout the world to help provide us with the information that allows us to do this.

What kind of skills are the most important for someone to have at the CIA?

It helps to be curious about the world outside of the United States. You'll be doing a lot of reading in most CIA jobs, and this curiosity helps keep you motivated. You also need to have good writing skills, strong critical thinking skills, and be comfortable speaking one-on-one to new people as well.

What did you like best about working there?

My favorite part about working at the CIA was getting to travel to places I would never imagine I'd get to visit. I also really enjoyed meeting with people who shared my interests—getting to develop ideas by sharing them and debating them with really smart people is a lot of fun, and a great learning experience!

What did you study in college, and where did you go?

I studied political science, and have both a bachelor of science and a master of arts degree in political science. My BS is from the University of Nebraska at Kearney, and my MA is from Iowa State University.

What do you know now that you wish you had known at age ten?

I wish I knew that some of the things that seemed like the end of the world at age ten—fights with friends, dealing with bullies, or finding out a boy I liked didn't like me back—are things I would barely remember by the time I became an adult. I also wish I knew that I would like pumpkin pie as a grown-up. My mom told me I would and I thought she was crazy. Had I known, I would have tried it sooner and would have had so many more years enjoying it. :)

What is the one best piece of advice you have for young girls who will be going to high school, college, and joining the workforce in the next decade or so?

Don't let the mean girls and bullies get to you. They won't matter at all in a few years, and I've discovered they rarely succeed past high school. Also, study hard, because grades do matter and the study habits you build now will serve you well in high school and college. If you leave high school not knowing exactly what you want to do with your life, don't worry! Take some college classes that interest you, seek out interactions with professors, and pursue things you are passionate about. You'll discover pretty quickly what it is you were meant to do! As you enter the workforce, try not to take yourself too seriously. You'll make mistakes—we all have. Mistakes are rarely fatal, and usually the only person who remembers them the next day is you. You'll have a lot less stress if you can learn to correct mistakes and move on quickly.

Is there a quote, an inspirational thought, or anything like that that motivates you each day?

A verse of Scripture from Micah 6:8: "What does the Lord require of you? To do justly, love mercy, and walk humbly with your God."

> "Don't let the mean girls and bullies get to you. They won't matter at all in a few years, and I've discovered they rarely succeed past high school."
>
> —Gail Helt

now

THEN

Dr. Anne Kress

President, Northern Virginia Community College

📍 **Annandale, Virginia**

With some eighty thousand students, Northern Virginia Community College is one of the largest community colleges in the United States.

Hello! What is a community college, and what does the president of a college do?

Community colleges provide access to higher education to anyone with a high school diploma. They were created to ensure that everyone has the opportunity to attend college, so tuition at community colleges is much lower (usually 40 percent to 50 percent) than the tuition at a university. Most students will also find a community college campus near where they live, so they commute to attend class rather than living in dorms or residence halls. In most other ways, community colleges mirror four-year colleges: faculty qualifications, student services, student life, arts and cultural programs, and athletics. Because community colleges reflect the communities they serve, their student enrollment is often more diverse than that found at most four-year colleges and universities, and the colleges offer a full range of services and programming to support equity in student success. In addition to providing preparation for transfer to a four-year college or university, community colleges offer career and workforce education in areas such as healthcare, information technology, the trades, and hospitality.

The president is the chief executive officer of the community college. I am responsible for setting the vision, fulfilling the mission, and implementing the community college's strategic plan—typically all of these center on advancing student success and serving and partnering with the local community. The president is the key decision maker on most matters, including budget. Most often, the president tracks the success of the community college by looking at measures like student success, graduation, and transfer to university or employment. The president is also tasked with raising funds to support student scholarships, build new facilities, and start or grow programs. The president is the public "face" of the community college and is expected to meet regularly with faculty, staff, and students as well as business leaders and elected officials. The president also advocates for the college's students, faculty, and staff to ensure they get the funding they need at the local, state, and federal level.

What skills are the most important for someone in your role to know?

A community college president must be an excellent communicator. She must also be able to think critically and creatively about complex problems, be able to build and lead a strong team, and be flexible and collaborative. Because of the unique open access mission of community colleges, a president must understand the needs of students, value diversity and inclusion, and be a powerful advocate. Finally, because so much of a president's work concerns budget and data, she must be comfortable with numbers and understand how to make informed decisions on tight timelines.

What do you like best about being a college president?

I am a true believer in the community college mission, in the role that we play in providing access to opportunity to those who might otherwise never get to attend college. So, our mission is my passion. Because of this, meeting with students and helping them succeed is what I like best about my role. It's what keeps me going. My favorite day every year is commencement—knowing how much our students have overcome to get to that stage is humbling and inspiring. It's an honor to shake their hands and offer my congratulations. I cry with joy and pride every time.

What did you study in college, and where did you go?

When I was ten, I never imagined that I would attend college, let alone become a community college president. I am the first in my family to earn a college degree. I attended the University of Florida on an honors scholarship to earn my bachelor's in finance, then earned a second bachelor's in English and a master's in English from UF. After working at a community college for over a decade, I went back to the University of Florida when my two children were toddlers and earned my PhD in higher education administration.

What do you know now that you wish you had known at age ten?

I was very shy when I was ten. I was smart but rarely spoke in class and kept to myself. Now I know the importance of finding and using one's voice. I would tell my ten-year-old self to push past her shyness and be brave enough to share her ideas. As I grew older, I also learned how important it is to find mentors and champions—and how willing people are to help and provide advice. So, I would push my younger self to connect with great role models and mentors and tell her not to be afraid of reaching out. Looking back, I see that I wasted so much energy being fearful and so much time by trying to go it alone. So, I'd tell ten-year-old Anne, speak up and find your squad!

What is the one best piece of advice you have for young girls who will be going to high school, college, and joining the workforce in the next decade or so?

One thing I've learned over time is that it's better to have an advocate than a cheerleader. An advocate helps you advance while being honest with you about what that's going to take.

A cheerleader cheers. So, my advice would be to find advocates who care about you and your success and listen equally to their kind praise and tough love. And thank them for both.

Is there a quote, an inspirational thought, or anything like that that motivates you each day?

Time and time again, I come back to a quote attributed to Helen Keller: "Alone we can do so little; together we can do so much."

I also reflect on the words of one of my graduate school professors. Though we disagreed on almost everything, he had nominated one of my papers for an award. (It won.) I tried to explain to him why he misunderstood the paper, and he stopped me, saying, "Ms. Kress, when someone does something nice for you, the best course of action is usually just to say, 'Thank you,' and leave." Always say "thank you," and you can never say it enough.

> "Alone we can do so little; together we can do so much."
>
> —Helen Keller

now

THEN

Lauren Strawderman

Third-Grade Teacher
📍 **Bridgewater, Virginia**

Knowledge, wisdom, curiosity—
our teachers give us all this
and so much more!

Hello! You are a third-grade school teacher. Where do you teach and how long have you been doing it?

I've been a third-grade teacher in Rockingham County for the last thirty-one years. That's well over half my life! My school is in Bridgewater, Virginia, in the Shenandoah Valley.

What skills are the most important for you to know to be a teacher?

Teachers need to be organized and creative. It helps to be tech-savvy and outgoing. More importantly, teachers need to be effective communicators, both in speaking and listening. Some of my students spend more waking hours with me than with their parents on a daily basis. I may be one of the only adults they can talk to, so I want them to know that when they need to talk, I'm listening. I need to be consistently fair and constantly patient. Every student (and family) is doing the best that they can. It's a teacher's job to help students love learning and to have faith that they can reach their goals. We have to give them the tools they need to succeed through skills and a positive attitude. Teachers set the example.

What do you like best about your job?

I love the relationships I build with my students and seeing them grow as learners and as people throughout the year. I love building a classroom community and seeing my students help each other with what we're learning. I love watching the progress they make during the year, becoming more independent and confident. Basically, I love the kids. That's what it's all about.

What did you study in college, and where did you go?

I have known I wanted to be a teacher since middle school. I went to Mary Baldwin University and majored in elementary education/psychology.

What do you know now that you wish you had known at age ten?

People may ask you what you want to be when you grow up. You will "be" many things in the course of your life, not just what you do for a job. You don't have to wait until then to "be" or to do what gives you joy. If that changes (and it will), change with it. Be you, now!

What is the one best piece of advice you have for young girls who will be going to high school, college, and joining the workforce in the next decade or so?

The world needs you and your unique gifts and perspective. Don't try to be someone else, be the best you that you can be. Be true to yourself and you will find yourself in the place you were meant to be.

Is there a quote, an inspirational thought, or anything like that that motivates you each day?

They won't care how much you know until they know how much you care.

"The world needs you and your unique gifts and perspective. Don't try to be someone else..."

—Lauren Strawderman

Energy

now

THEN

Noël Bakhtian

Director of Tech Acceleration, Bezos Earth Fund*

📍 Oakland, California

Science means "to know." It is the gathering of knowledge, facts, or principles gained through study, observation, and/or experimentation.

At the time of our interview, Noël was Executive Director of the Berkeley Lab Energy Storage Center at the Lawrence Berkeley National Laboratory (and formerly Senior Policy Advisor at the White House Office of Science and Technology Policy).

Hello! You were the executive director of the Berkeley Lab Energy Storage Center at the Lawrence Berkeley National Laboratory. What is that? And what do you do?

Berkeley Lab is one of the seventeen national labs across the country owned by the U.S. Department of Energy. We have thousands of brilliant people and billions of dollars of unique equipment that help us do research to accelerate progress on national priorities like clean energy! As the first Executive Director of the Berkeley Lab Energy Storage Center, my role is to harness, guide, and galvanize the expertise, capabilities, and innovation of over two hundred researchers to create new science, technology, and policy energy storage solutions. Our work, together with partners around the world, is changing the power grid, transportation, buildings, manufacturing, and communities!

What skills are the most important for you to know to do your job?

1) Curiosity. By talking to as many researchers as I can and learning about their work, it helps me create a framework through the Center to support them and enable all their work to be bigger than the sum of the parts.

2) Connecting. I've always loved connecting ideas and connecting people. In my recent roles, I've found that driving toward a collaborative and in-

clusive process leads to the most interesting and impactful solutions.

3) Communication. Being able to communicate complex concepts (for example, science and technology) to a general audience can be incredibly powerful.

What do you like best about your job?

I love being surrounded by and learning from brilliant, passionate people who want to change the world.

What did you study in college, and where did you go?

In high school, I loved math and science, and everyone told me I would love engineering. I wasn't sure exactly what that was yet, so I picked a school that is really good at both liberal arts and engineering: Duke University. I studied mechanical engineering and physics to get a good grounding, and then I went on to do my graduate studies in aeronautical engineering, because I've always loved space and wanted to work at NASA.

(Note: Noël also earned master's degrees at Stanford University and University of Cambridge in England, where she was a Churchill Scholar, and a PhD from Stanford.)

What do you know now that you wish you had known at age ten?

It's OK to take risks and say yes and try things that are scary! We only live once, and it goes by so fast—so dream big and go for it!

What is the one best piece of advice you have for young girls who will be going to high school, college, and joining the workforce in the next decade or so?

It's OK not to know what you want to be when you grow up. At any point in my career, if you had told me what I would be doing in five years, I would have laughed you out of the room! But if you love what you're doing, you'll work hard at it, and doors will open for you and you will have incredible adventures!

Is there a quote, an inspirational thought, or anything like that that motivates you each day?

"Shoot for the moon. Even if you miss, you'll land among the stars." —Norman Vincent Peale
Also: *"Do, or do not. There is no try." —Yoda* :)

Thank you very much!!

Thank YOU for what you're doing for other little girls and young women.

> "I love being surrounded by and learning from brilliant, passionate people who want to change the world."
>
> —Noël Bakhtian

now

THEN

Mei Cai

Director, Battery Cell Systems Research, General Motors Research & Development

📍 **Warren, Michigan**

Automakers the world over are rapidly shifting from gasoline-powered cars to electric cars— and batteries are key!

Hello! You are the Director of Battery Cell Systems Research, General Motors R&D. That sounds very exciting! Please tell me what that means and what you do.

My team is responsible for identifying, developing, and implementing battery technology that is better for the environment and less expensive to make than older versions, while also meeting General Motors's energy density goals. I lead a team of thirty scientists who work every day to discover new battery technology innovations.

What skills are the most important for you to know to do your job?

There are five big ones:

- Problem solving: identifying issues and quickly finding solutions
- Analytical skills: knowing how to solve problems and analyze data
- Technical skills: having a strong math, physics, chemistry, and engineering skill set
- Communication skills: the ability to discuss your ideas with people who are not familiar with your work
- Teamwork: collaborating with teams in many different areas of the company

What do you like best about your job?

I love to see technology continue to improve, and I am thankful that GM provides a strong platform to practice every aspect of innovation, from coming up with new ideas, to technology development, to real life uses of our discoveries.

101

What did you study in college, and where did you go?

I earned a bachelor's degree in chemical engineering from Tsinghua University in China, and I earned my master's and doctorate degrees in chemical engineering from Wayne State University in Detroit, Michigan.

What do you know now that you wish you had known at age ten?

I wish I knew when I was young exactly what I wanted to do with my career so I could take advice from people in my current career field.

What is the one best piece of advice you have for young girls who will be going to high school, college, and joining the workforce in the next decade or so?

Dream big and don't be afraid to go outside of your comfort zone.

Can you tell me about a professional or personal setback you had, how you overcame it, and what you learned from it?

When I was young, I was never a good student, especially in elementary school. In the traditional Chinese educational system, only students that obeyed the teacher and their superiors were defined as good students. I was never good at listening to instruction and frequently disobeyed authority. Because of that, I was labeled as a "bad kid." I was always in the bottom 20 percent of my class. Once I was in fifth grade, I had a new literature teacher, and she was the one who really changed my life. She saw my potential and helped me to become a leader. Her decision ignited the fire in me to become a better student. I saw that I could realize my potential, and I could change my behavior. Later, my academics improved because I started to pay attention in class. Within one year, my grade went to the top 10 percent.

What I learned is you should always be your best self and believe in your capabilities.

Is there a quote, an inspirational thought, or anything like that that motivates you each day?

"Shoot for the moon. Even if you miss, you'll land among the stars." —*Norman Vincent Peale*

"Dream big and don't be afraid to go outside of your comfort zone."

—Mei Cai

Environment and Sustainability

now

THEN

Amy Berry

Chief Executive
Officer, Tahoe Fund

📍 Incline Village, Nevada

Protecting our earth and
our environment.

You are the CEO of the Tahoe Fund. What is the Tahoe Fund, and what do you do?

The Tahoe Fund is a nonprofit that uses the power of philanthropy to improve the Lake Tahoe environment for all to enjoy. As the CEO, my job is to find great projects that will improve the environment and then to find generous people to help fund them.

What skills and knowledge do you need to have to do your job?

- Environmental issues: I have to understand the critical environmental issues impacting Lake Tahoe so that I can help find projects that will solve those issues.
- Relationship building: Every project we work on is a collaboration, so it is important that I develop strong relationships with the partners that we are doing projects with. I also have to ask people to generously donate to these projects, and the best way to ask someone for money is after you have built a good relationship that is rooted in trust.
- Storytelling: It is my job to raise the money for these projects, but they aren't always very appealing on the surface. It is important to tell the story of the project—who is doing, how it will make things better, who will benefit—in a compelling way that inspires people to support it.
- Fundraising: At the end of the day, if we don't raise the money to do the projects, they won't get done. It is my job to build compelling campaigns for our work so that people are inspired to donate.

What do you like best about your job?

I get to work with amazing people while really making a difference for the Lake Tahoe community. I can walk on a new path and know that because of the Tahoe Fund, that path is there. It is very rewarding.

What did you study in college, and where did you go?

I majored in American civilization at Brown University. I learned a lot about our country along with excellent critical thinking and communication skills.

What do you know now that you wish you had known at age ten?

That it's okay if you don't know what you want to do when you graduate from college. You can go try a lot of different things until the thing that brings you the most excitement, energy, and joy shows itself. Those prior experiences build upon each other to create a skill set that will ultimately make you successful at what you really want to do. Also, that I would eventually be more than five feet tall!

What is the one best piece of advice you have for girls who will be going to high school, college, and joining the workforce in the next decade or so?

It is okay if you don't know what you want to do. Just focus on what excites you. Find your passion. There will be a job or a career for you if you are excited about it. It is okay to try different things to find the one thing you really want to focus on.

Tell me about a personal or professional failure or setback you encountered. How did you overcome it, and what did you learn from it?

My senior year in college I was on the sailing team. Our women's team was incredible. We won every regatta. We were so good that we were the first all-women's team to compete in the Varsity/co-ed division. We had to fight really hard to compete against the boys, who were usually bigger and stronger. At the Women's National Championships, I was penalized for doing something a younger sailor thought was illegal. It was a technique used by everyone in the co-ed division, but was a little advanced for the women's fleet she was used to sailing in. It was really a judgment call, and unfortunately the judges sided with her. We ended up second at Nationals, and I was devastated. Almost twenty-five years later I am still mad about it. But I made a vow that day that forever onward I would always compete at the Varsity level, where pushing the limits was welcomed and encouraged. It was a great life lesson. It is easy to hang out in the lower level and win, but it is important to always push to be in the highest level and to compete to win at that level.

Is there a quote, an inspirational thought, or anything like that that motivates you each day?

I have Shel Silverstein's poem, "Listen to the Mustn'ts" on my wall. You should google it!

Is there anything you would like to add that we are not asking here?

I mentioned it above, but I really think success comes from passion. Just like in school where you tend to do the best in the subjects you like the most, you will be the most successful doing something you love. It isn't always obvious what that is, so it is okay to explore a bit to find it. But once you find it, put your all into it.

> "It is important to always push to be at the highest level and to compete to win at that level."
>
> —Amy Berry

now

THEN

Cora Snyder

Senior Researcher, Pacific Institute

📍 Oakland, California

Will we have enough water?

Hello! You are a senior researcher at the Pacific Institute. What is the Pacific Institute, and what does a senior researcher do? Please tell me about your job.

The Pacific Institute is a nonprofit organization focused on water sustainability research. Our mission is to create and advance solutions to the world's most pressing water challenges. At the Pacific Institute, I study crises like the California drought and global climate change and work with others to help solve them.

What skills are the most important for you to know to be a water researcher?

I need to know a lot about the science behind climate change and droughts. I also need strong writing, speaking, and storytelling skills, so that I can collaborate well with others and help people understand the importance of the issues that I work on.

What do you like best about your job?

I like working on water issues because water is such a vital resource, and everyone has a personal relationship with water. I also like having a job that allows me to make a positive difference in the world.

What did you study in college?

I went to undergraduate and graduate school at the University of California, Santa Barbara. I got my bachelor's degree in environmental studies and my master's degree in environmental science and management.

What do you know now that you wish you had known at age ten?

Making mistakes is okay. It never feels good, but it's how you learn. I got teased in school for being a "teacher's pet" and a "nerd" because I loved school and loved to learn. If that's you, it is nothing to be ashamed of! In fact, it's something to be proud of. Also, I wish I knew that you have to believe in yourself! No matter who you are, what you look like, what you are interested in, you have something special to share and contribute to the world.

What is the one best piece of advice you have for young girls who will be going to high school, college, and joining the workforce in the next decade or so?

Be assertive and kind. Be confident and humble. Now more than ever, the world needs the unique ability of women and girls to be caring and empathetic and solve complicated problems.

Can you tell me about a professional or personal setback you had, how you overcame it, and what you learned from it?

I was always an "A" student throughout my school career, but in graduate school I had to take some highly technical courses that were super hard for me. In one particularly difficult class, I got a "D" on my midterm. It was the lowest grade I'd ever gotten in my life, and I was shocked and defeated. I didn't want to tell any of my friends or classmates because I was so embarrassed. After a few days of feeling sorry for myself and calling my mom on the phone, I swallowed my pride and went to see the class TA (teacher's assistant). He kindly walked through the entire test with me and helped me understand what I had done wrong, and how to do it correctly. I couldn't change my grade on that test, but I was very dedicated the rest of the class and went to get help from the TA several more times, and I ended up with a "B" in the class. I've never been so proud to get a "B"! That experience taught me that sometimes you fail, and it might feel like the end of your career or success, but it's just part of the journey. It also taught me the importance of asking for extra help when you need it, and not letting your pride get in the way.

Is there a quote, an inspirational thought, or anything like that that motivates you each day?

"There are only two ways to live your life. One is as though nothing is a miracle. The other is as though everything is a miracle." —Albert Einstein

"When you want something, all the universe conspires in helping you achieve it." —Paulo Coelho

> "Making mistakes is okay. It never feels good, but it's how you learn."
>
> —Cora Snyder

Government Service

now

THEN

Carmela Conroy

 Foreign Service Officer (ret.),
U.S. Department of State;
Democratic Party Chair

📍 Spokane County, Washington

Representing America to the rest of the world.

Hello! You worked for the U.S. State Department for many years and were a Foreign Service Officer and a U.S. diplomat. Tell me what the State Department is and what a diplomat does.

The U.S. Department of State is the part of the U.S. government that discusses international issues with other countries' governments. Diplomats are the people within the Department of State who do that work.

For example, diplomats discuss the rules for Americans to visit other countries, or for people from other countries to visit the United States. Diplomats discuss whether and how we can sell or buy things like blueberries, books, and bicycles to and from other countries. Diplomats discuss how we can stop the climate change crisis together, because no one country can fix the problem.

What skills are the most important for a diplomat to know?

Diplomats have to be good listeners, and ask good questions. Diplomats must make sure that they understand what the people on the other side want, and also that those people understand what America wants.

Diplomats must gather good information and think carefully about how to apply it. History books help us understand what has happened in the past between the United States and other countries. Books about art and culture help us find beauty in human expression. Books about ethics, about distinguishing between right and wrong, help us remember there's a difference between what we can do and what we should do.

What did you like best about being a diplomat?

It is an amazing honor to be welcomed as a stranger into peoples' homes. People living in different cultures have different kinds of events to celebrate important things in their lives. Everywhere, from New Zealand to Norway, people treasure the birth of a baby, the joining of a couple in a lifelong partnership, and the passing from this world to the next. Many people who welcomed me into their homes are still friends years later.

It is also an honor to represent the United States. When Americans get sick or get into trouble in other countries, diplomats help keep them safe. Diplomats share American music, and ideas about all people being created equal, and baseball and basketball with people in other countries. Diplomats also have to have difficult conversations before, during, and after wars, when people are hurt and angry. Sometimes it is hard or even scary. When it gets like that, it helps me to remember what my parents taught me about the importance of doing the right thing and being brave.

What did you study in college, and where did you go?

Before I became a diplomat, I studied international relations and law at the University of Washington in Seattle. I also studied the Japanese language in Seattle, Tokyo, and Palo Alto. After joining the State Department, I kept studying Japanese, and also studied some Norwegian and a little bit of Dari, or Afghan Persian. I also got to go to the U.S. Naval War College in Newport, Rhode Island, for a year of national security studies.

What do you know now that you wish you had known at age ten?

I wish I had known how welcoming the world would be, and that it's okay to ask for help, and it's also okay to make mistakes.

What is the one best piece of advice you have for young girls who will be going to high school, college, and joining the workforce in the next decade or so?

Study hard, work hard, and have fun. If the first work you find isn't right for you, keep looking around to find what is. Believe your own eyes and heart. Most people change jobs many times as adults, so don't worry if you don't know what you want to be when you grow up. Maybe you'll get to do many different things. Since I was ten years old, I have been a student, a fast-food worker, a secretary, a teacher, a lawyer, and a diplomat. I wonder what I'm going to be next!

Is there a quote, an inspirational thought, or anything like that that motivates you each day?

I am happiest when I begin and end each day thinking about what makes me feel grateful. I'm grateful for my dog. For my warm bed. For sunflowers. Even when bad things happen, there's something for which I'm thankful. Some people call this counting their blessings.

> **"I am happiest when I begin and end each day thinking about what makes me feel grateful."**
>
> —Carmela Conroy

now

THEN

Carmen Medina

 Deputy Director, Central Intelligence Agency (ret.); Co-Author, *Rebels at Work: A Handbook for Leading Change from Within*

📍 Virginia

Keeping America safe!

You spent thirty-two years in the U.S. intelligence community. Wow! Please tell young girls what that's like and what you did (without being too revealing!).

Working at the CIA in many ways is like working at any large organization or business. You have all the ups and downs of being in a bureaucracy, but at CIA you gain from the advantage of a compelling mission. The CIA hires all sorts of people: analytic types, extroverts, business minds, doctors, nurses, data scientists, you'd be amazed.

What skills were the most important for you to do your job(s)?

Critical thinking skills, clear, concise writing, and strong verbal communications skills. Also lots and lots of emotional intelligence and ability to learn continuously.

What did you like best about your job(s)?

I liked the combination of grappling with difficult questions and contributing to the growth of colleagues while working in teams.

What did you study in college, and where did you go?

I ended up taking courses at five different colleges/universities (including Texas Tech, University of Texas at El Paso, Prince George's Community College). My degree in government was from Catholic University in DC. I also went to Georgetown University for graduate school in the school of foreign service.

What do you know now that you wish you had known at age ten?

What you should learn as you get older is that life is more complex than you think it is, and yet—paradoxically—also more simple. Issues are complex and trying to control outcomes is foolish—so don't be a perfectionist. But the best way to navigate all this complexity is by sticking to some basic principles that work for you. I have three: Be curious about everything. Never embarrass other people. Talk as little about yourself as possible (which I am breaking by answering your questions).

What is the one best piece of advice you have for young girls who will be going to high school, college, and joining the workforce in the next decade or so?

Mine is very practical. Think about the expected salary of the profession you are aiming for. If you want to work for the government or an NGO (non-governmental organization) for example, you can't expect a huge salary, so don't take on excessive college debt.

Is there a quote, an inspirational thought, or anything like that that motivates you each day?

"Optimism is the greatest act of rebellion."

Can you tell me about a professional or personal setback you had, how you overcame it, and what you learned from it?

I was reassigned from a job I loved because I was told I wasn't "hard" enough as a senior manager. In the end it was a blessing because it led me to retire from the CIA earlier than I might have otherwise and has allowed me to have a full second career. The experience reaffirmed my view that I didn't ever want to be a "hard" manager.

Is there anything you would like to add that we are not asking here?

Success is a byproduct of hard work, resilience, generosity, and luck. It should never be your destination.

> "Be curious about everything; Never embarrass other people; Talk as little about yourself as possible (which I am breaking by answering your questions)."
>
> —Carmen Medina

now

THEN

with her brother

Ileana Ros-Lehtinen

Fifteen-Term Congresswoman from Florida (1989–2019); Senior Advisor on Public Policy, Akin Gump Strauss Hauer & Feld

📍 **Pinecrest, Florida**

Representing citizens in Congress.

Hello! You represented Florida in Congress for thirty years! What was that like, and what do you do now?

My nearly thirty years in Congress brought me a great deal of pride and satisfaction. Every time I saw the Capitol dome, it reinvigorated and inspired me to continue to fight for the issues that were important to my district and to me. I was an eight-year-old Cuban refugee who spoke no English when I arrived in the U.S. The greatness and generosity of the United States allowed me the honor of becoming the first Hispanic woman elected to Congress.

During my time serving in the People's House, the greatest joy and professional satisfaction came from helping my community. Helping the senior citizens navigate the maze of the Social Security and Medicare systems, or helping individuals with their immigration status, honoring our veterans by assisting with their VA claims or replacing lost medals, these were the individual cases where I could make a real difference. Introducing and passing legislation that impacts many individuals was also a source of great pride.

Public service is about helping people, and throughout my career that has been my focus. I was blessed not only with hard-working staffers who went the extra mile every day, but I was able to collaborate with many of my colleagues from both sides of the aisle to pass meaningful legislation.

As life teaches us, there is a time for everything, and when I decided that my time in Congress had been completed, I changed from serving constituents to serving clients.

I am currently a Senior Advisor on Public Policy for the international law firm of Akin Gump Strauss Hauer & Feld. In addition to providing traditional legal services to clients, both individuals and corporations, our firm helps clients by advocating or lobbying for or against potential legislation that impacts their industry. My job is to help my clients through my professional network as a former member of Congress to ensure that my client's message regarding a proposed bill is clear and reaches the appropriate audience.

What skills are the most important for you to know to do your job?

People skills are the most important. In Congress, my network of connections and friends grew because I made a concentrated effort to engage and get along with my colleagues from both sides of the aisle. In my current job, this has helped me to advocate for my clients' needs.

What do you like best about your job?

My public service career started in 1982 in the Florida House of Representatives. Prior to that, I was the principal of a private grade-school in South Florida. I have always enjoyed helping people. Whether it was helping my students, helping my constituents, or now helping my clients, being of assistance is what I like most.

What did you study in college, and where did you go?

I received my Associate in Arts from Miami Dade College and then attended Florida International University, where I obtained both my bachelor's and master's in arts degrees. In 2004, while a member of Congress, I completed my doctorate in education at the University of Miami.

What do you know now that you wish you had known at age ten?

When you are young, sometimes you want to have everything. As you grow and garner experience, you realize you can have all that you want—family- and career-wise—just maybe not all on the same day. You must make choices, and sometimes family will come first and other times your career comes first.

What is the one best piece of advice you have for young girls who will be going to high school, college, and joining the workforce in the next decade or so?

Hard work and perseverance do pay off. Be kind to people. Smile and choose to be happy! Be your own advocate. Craft your message and stick with it. Be the catalyst of change that you want to see in the world or in your community. One person—you—can make a difference.

Is there a quote, an inspirational thought, or anything like that that motivates you each day?

As a public servant, I was blessed to meet with many heads of states, presidents, and famous individuals, but the one that made a lasting impact on me was Mother Teresa. She was a soft-spoken woman, and in meeting and speaking with her, it showed me that you can be one humble person, but still effect great change in the world.

Can you tell me about a professional or personal setback you had, how you overcame it, and what you learned from it?

Life is a compilation of successes and setbacks. I enjoy successful moments, whether they are personal or professional, and I face setbacks, also both personal and career, with the attitude that tomorrow can be better. Look at the problem and the obstacle and determine why you were not successful and then tackle it from a different angle.

Is there anything you would like to add that we are not asking here, Congresswoman?

In the times we are living, it is important to foster tolerance and acceptance of individuals at every turn in life. Kindness is not costly—practice it as much as you can in everyday situations.

> "Be kind to people. Smile and choose to be happy! Be your own advocate."
>
> —Ileana Ros-Lehtinen

Journalism

now

Photo by The New York Times

THEN

Maureen Dowd

 Pulitzer Prize–
Winning Columnist,
The New York Times

📍 **Washington, D.C.**

Writing about interesting
people, ideas, and trends.

Hello! You are a columnist for *The New York Times*! Wow! Tell me about your job.

When I got a column at *The New York Times* in 1995, there had not been very many women columnists, and that remained true for many years after I got my column, though I often complained publicly about it. When I first got into journalism in 1975—and for a long time after—the prevailing male attitude about a woman writing at magazines and newspapers seemed to be summed up by Samuel Johnson's line, "Sir, a woman's preaching is like a dog's walking on his hind legs. It is not done well; but you are surprised to find it done at all."

If you want to know how ridiculous that was, simply pick up a book by Dorothy Parker or Joan Didion or Jane Austen or Edith Wharton.

I found it hard to write opinion journalism, much harder than reporting stories. But once you accept a job, you have to make sure you do it as well as you can. I think it took *Times* readers a while to adjust to the idea that I was not writing a column from the left or the right. It was the first time there was a political column at the paper that did not have a definite red or blue ideological slant. Democrats got mad at me sometimes, and Republicans—including my family!—got mad at me other times. I've been called an "equal opportunity" critic.

There is a lot of pressure on high-profile columnists, especially women, in the Twitter age. So, you have to have "a skin as thick as a rhinoceros hide," as Eleanor Roosevelt said, to be out in the arena. I am extremely sensitive and get hurt easily; I've been like that since I was a child. So my family thinks it's hilarious that I ended up in a profession that can get as vindictive as a *Godfather* movie!

My friend Mary McGrory, a famous Pulitzer Prize–winning liberal columnist who worked with me at *The Washington Star* and later at *The Washington Post*, used to say when you entered a room where you didn't know anyone, and you had to work the room, just "Approach the shrimp bowl like you own it." Fake it 'til you make it!

What skills are the most important for you to know to do your job?

If you want to improve your writing, follow this advice: Just make sure that you have taken out every extraneous word. Make sure every sentence is clear and simple, so that the reader is lured onto the next sentence. Try to make your first and last sentences snappy, and then fact-check it to make sure all the punctuation and grammar and facts are correct. If you do all that, you may not be F. Scott Fitzgerald, but you will be very readable!

What do you like best about being a columnist?

I like the fact that I am my own boss and can decide what to write about and where to travel. That kind of autonomy is fun.

What did you study in college, and where did you go?

I went to Catholic schools all the way through: convent-bred! I graduated from Catholic University with a BA in English literature. And now I'm getting my master's in English literature at Columbia University. It's never too late to go back to school!

What do you know now that you wish you had known at age ten?

Lots of things! I always knew not to smoke and I'm proud of that; it's a silly vice. I learned the hard way in my job that the best safety net is yourself. Never rely on others to do what you can do yourself. Do your own fact-checking. And trust your own judgment on any work that you are responsible for. If your name is on it, you will be blamed if something goes wrong, not anyone else behind the scenes. As my Irish dad used to say, "Never bolt the door with a boiled carrot."

What is the one best piece of advice you have for young girls who will be going to high school, college, and joining the workforce in the next decade or so?

Don't be a victim. Stand up for yourself. As I like to say, the minute you settle for less than you deserve, you get even less than you settled for. And go for opportunities; don't put off making a leap because you are afraid. Fear can be your friend. As a friend of mine used to say, "Jump on it before it's not there to jump on."

Is there a quote, an inspirational thought, or anything like that that motivates you each day?

My mom, my role model, used to say: never let yourself dwell on the bad stuff that happens. "When blue, wear red," she always said. A red piece of clothing, a red lipstick, whatever, just to remind yourself to stay positive.

Is there anything I'm not asking that you'd like to add?

I get attacked all the time in my job. Again, my mom used to say about unfair critics, "Put out a saucer of milk for them." Meaning, they were being catty, and possibly jealous, and they should be ignored. You are the leading lady in your own movie. Don't let others define you.

> "The minute you settle for less than you deserve, you get even less than you settled for."
>
> —Maureen Dowd

now

THEN

Norah O'Donnell

Anchor,
CBS Evening News

♀ Washington, D.C.

Delivering the news to millions of Americans!

Hello! You are the anchor for the CBS Evening News. Wow! Please tell me about your job.

I think being the anchor of the *CBS Evening News* is one of the proudest moments of my career. You know, it is a profound responsibility to anchor the *CBS Evening News*. There are more than five million Americans who tune in every night to watch the broadcast. And what we try to do is original reporting and great storytelling. And I like to say that I anchor the broadcast like I try to play golf and just hit the ball right down the middle, you know, we're not a show that's full of opinion. We're about objective reporting. So people can turn to the *CBS Evening News* to get facts and to try and get understanding about a lot of complex issues that happen every single day.

What skills are most important for you to know to do your job?

Asking good questions is very important. You know, 95 percent of getting the right answer is asking the right question and making sure you listen. And so, in my job, I spend a lot of time listening to people. And I spend a lot of time actually thinking about the right kinds of questions to ask people in order to help further understanding. I think this is one of the things that we're not taught a lot as younger people. People are taught all kinds of different skills. But listening is an incredibly important skill—actively listening to what people are saying and then asking the proper follow-up question, so that you can really learn something, or in the case of a journalist, maybe break some news, because people reveal a lot about themselves in their jobs, when they talk about that when you interview them.

What do you like best about your job?

The best part about my job is that I get to do something new every single day and I get to meet the most fascinating people in the world. As a journalist, I get to interview presidents, prime ministers, princes, as well as people who are leaders in their field in science, the arts, or who are incredible authors. I have a great sense of curiosity about things, about people, and about the world. And so being a journalist is one of the best ways to feed that curiosity. The other great thing about my job is the people I work with. A lot of my coworkers are also people who are very curious and interested in the world and people around them. So we spend a lot of time just talking about the news, what's happening in the news, and all the exciting things that are happening, not only in America, but around the world. And so that makes me think the field of journalism is very exciting, and it's never boring. And no two days are the same, which is pretty cool too.

What did you study in college, and where did you go?

I went to Georgetown University and I majored in philosophy with a minor in English. And one of the reasons that I really liked philosophy was because it was the opportunity to read about virtues and values and ethics. But also to write a lot of papers, and I really enjoy reading and writing. So what really fit my interest level was being a philosophy major. And I think I learned a lot. If you look at the ancient philosophers like Aristotle or Plato, they talk a lot about the value of listening, learning, and curiosity, which really fit with my goal of being a journalist.

Very interesting. Okay. What do you know now that you wish you had known at age ten?

You know, this is a very good question, Julia. And I was thinking a lot about it. What I wish that I knew when I was ten was the importance of nourishing your relationships, nourishing your intellect, and nourishing your curiosity. You know, I am now forty-eight years old. I am still friends with all the girls that I knew when I was ten years old and then in middle school and high school when growing up in San Antonio, Texas. And I think having long-lasting friendships is incredibly important to one's mental health and stability. And so I always say that the quality of your life is built on your relationships. So nourish your relationships, not only your friendships, but your professional relationships because they will come in handy throughout your entire career. You know, when I look back, I wish that I had spent more time studying history, more time traveling around the world, because all these things just become more and more helpful as you get older.

What is the one best piece of advice you have for young girls?

I think this is an important question as well. I think it is that you should develop a skill set. I think, historically, women have had trouble reaching the upper echelons [levels] in certain fields because they don't have specific skill sets. If you look at the areas where women have achieved a lot, they're in the fields where they have, like I said, specific skill sets. Like in medicine, that's a specific skill set where you're judged more objectively on your skills. Law is a specific skill set, and while yes, we've seen women make it to the Supreme Court of the

United States of America, it's still in small numbers. And few women have made it to Fortune 500 CEOs, even though they have a specific skill set in terms of finance. And so I really do think that this is one of the things that is not directed enough at young women.

Building skill sets in a certain field is very important. And also I would add to develop a specific expertise in a sport or athletic endeavor.

I also believe that having an expertise in sports is important because it is closely tied with confidence. You know, being part of a team in sports, you learn very easily that you can lose and then you can go back and win again. Losing and defeat is just a step in the journey.

I really feel very strongly that preparation builds confidence and confidence builds success. And so what are the ways, you know, you can prepare and prepare and prepare? But how do you build confidence? It's multifaceted. And one of those is having a specific skill set and being really good at one thing that you can always lean back on and say, you know, I'm actually a really good piano player or I'm a really good golfer, and I spent a lot of time getting really good at that, which means I can do something else and get really good at it as well.

Terrific. Is there a quote or an inspirational thought or anything like that that motivates you every day?

Yes. I'm glad you asked me. One of the things that inspires me is this quote, which is "Believing in yourself is the ultimate superpower." If you believe in yourself, no one can take that away from you. And at the same time, though, you have to surround yourself with friends and a team of people who also believe in you, and that's the ultimate superpower.

Tell me about a professional or personal setback. How did you overcome it, and what did you learn from that?

Well, there's no doubt that I have had setbacks, but I just really don't remember them or dwell on them, and I just try and remove those things from my mindset. I try to just keep looking forward. But I really do kind of, I think, separate those into some section of my mind and flush it away. That's because if you start to dwell on the negative things, it can become all-consuming, and it's really just better to spend a lot of your energy moving forward.

Is there anything you'd like to add that we're not asking here?

I think it's important to nourish your intellect, because this will nourish your spirit. And that is what, at the end of the day, can lead to a happy life, which is the ultimate goal.

> "Believing in yourself is the ultimate superpower. If you believe in yourself, no one can take that away from you."
>
> —Norah O'Donnell

Legal and Law Enforcement

Jill Baker

 Criminal Defense Attorney, Minnesota Judicial Branch, Fifth Judicial District

📍 Mankato, Minnesota

The law is the bedrock of our nation.

Hello, Jill! You are a criminal defense attorney. What does a criminal defense attorney do?

A criminal defense attorney defends individuals who have been charged with a criminal offense. A criminal offense is generally a violation of law that could result in the loss of a person's "liberty." That means the person could be jailed, sent to prison, or otherwise have their freedoms taken away. Criminal offenses come in all types, from ordinary traffic tickets (speeding, driving while intoxicated), to more serious offenses such as assaulting another person. Criminal law is different than civil law, which includes things like contract disputes, real estate disputes, family law, and more. A person involved in a civil lawsuit—as opposed to a criminal complaint—generally does not have a right to have an attorney represent them. But when a person has been charged with a criminal offense, they do have the right to have an attorney help defend them. This is not because criminal law is more important than other law; it is because of the high stakes for a person charged with a criminal offense: they could go to prison.

A criminal defense attorney might work at the trial court level or at the appellate level. The trial court is the local court and it is where trials are held (among other proceedings). At the trial court level, a criminal defense attorney represents a person charged with one or more crimes. A lot can happen before a trial begins. The defense could bring what is known as a "motion"* before the court asking for particular things, such as Motions to Dismiss (throw the case out before the trial even begins), Motions to Exclude Evidence, and Motions to Impeach the government's witnesses. If the case does not

---

* A "motion" is what it's called when you want to ask the court for something—you "make a motion," either in writing or orally during court.

get resolved through such negotiations, the case then goes to trial. In a trial in the United States, the burden of proof is on the government, and not the person charged with the crime (the "defendant"). In other words, the government must prove that the defendant is guilty of the crime. The defendant does not ever have to prove his or her innocence, but the defense attorney will work up a theory of defense and generally use that theory to counter the government's witnesses and evidence against her.

A criminal defense attorney working at the appellate level is focused almost exclusively on written legal argument and oral argument to the court (although the trial court attorney also works in these areas). This is because when a case is at the appellate level, it generally means that any proceedings at the trial court level have already concluded. Because one party—either the prosecution or the defense—has a disagreement in some form with a decision made by the trial court, or by a jury, at the trial court level. The appellate court is a court of review, so to speak, that may permit the parties (the litigants) to further litigate and argue their cases. Typically, the actual defendant is not present at appellate court proceedings—just the attorneys for each side.

What kind of skills are the most important for a criminal defense attorney to know?

A strong knowledge of the law and a disciplined character are required to be an effective advocate (which is what an attorney is), for a criminal defendant. Attorneys aren't expected to know every little thing about a particular type of law as it applies to certain circumstances, but they are expected to diligently research and understand how the law applies to every case they work on. Defense attorneys should also have a good knowledge and familiarity with the court system they practice in.

Empathy and compassion for others is very helpful in the area of criminal law. This is because criminal defense attorneys often work with people who have difficult life circumstances, and who may be very afraid and unsure about what may happen to them. Understanding others and their point of view—how they may see the world—is a very helpful trait for a criminal defense attorney.

What do you like best about being a criminal defense attorney?

I like to litigate—meaning I like to argue in court. I have also practiced as a transactional attorney doing business, real estate, and tax law. In those areas, it would be rare for me to ever be in court. As a criminal defense attorney, I am in court just about every day, and many times all day. I also like the people involved in the practice, my clients (the defendants), and mostly all of the criminal defense attorneys I work with.

What did you study in college, and where did you go?

Minnesota State University in Mankato, MN. I studied political science and philosophy. I got my law degree from Mitchell Hamline School of Law (St. Paul, MN).

What is the one best piece of advice you have for young girls who will be going to high school, college, and joining the workforce in the next decade or so?

I would encourage you to work hard, but also to value your uniqueness and to recognize the value it offers the world.

Is there a quote, an inspirational thought, or anything like that that motivates you each day?

"The occasion is piled high with difficulty, and we must rise with the occasion..." —Abraham Lincoln

> **"I would encourage you to work hard, but also to value your uniqueness and to recognize the value it offers the world."**
>
> —Jill Baker

now

THEN

Subhashini Bollini

Civil Rights Attorney, Partner, Correia & Puth, PLLC

📍 Washington, D.C.

Helping citizens defend their rights!

Hello! You are a civil rights attorney. What does a civil rights attorney do? Please tell me about your job.

Our Constitution and certain federal, state, and local laws protect people from being treated unequally—which we call discrimination—because of certain characteristics like their race, skin color, gender, age, or disabilities.

Civil rights attorneys represent people who have been treated unfairly because of one or more of these characteristics. That term—civil rights—applies in many contexts in our lives. You might have learned in school about the Civil Rights Movement of the 1950s and '60s, which focused on civil rights in certain areas like education and voting. Civil rights lawyers at the time represented Black school children in Kansas who were told they couldn't attend school with White children and were instead forced to go to schools that didn't have equal funding, supplies, or facilities. Because of the work of those civil rights lawyers, the Supreme Court decided that Black children were not getting an equal education when they were forced to go to separate schools. Civil rights lawyers at that time also represented people in cases in which state or local governments in certain parts of the country denied people their constitutional right to vote because of their race or the color of their skin. Our country is changing, and we hope it is improving, so we don't have exactly those challenges today, but civil rights lawyers still do very important work to protect people's rights under the law.

I focus on protecting the civil rights of people in the workplace and ensuring that people have an equal opportunity to work and earn a living. Discrimination in the workplace includes things like being fired from a job, being paid less than others who do the same work, not being hired for a job that someone is qualified to do, or for people with disabilities, not being given the tools someone needs to help them do their job, like a desk that has room for a wheelchair to fit under it or software that reads words on a computer screen aloud to a person who is blind. Sometimes bosses and coworkers even bully people because of their disabilities, gender, race, or age, and if what they do is harmful enough, that type of behavior also violates the law.

I get calls and emails from people who believe they have been treated unfairly at work because of one of those characteristics I mentioned earlier: race, gender, age, or disability. Many people call me each week, so I cannot help everyone who calls, but I try to work with the other attorneys in my firm to help as many as we can. The people I represent are called my clients. If I can, I try to talk to my client's employer and explain to them why what they did violates the law. I try to give the employer a chance to do the right thing, and sometimes they do make things right by hiring someone or giving them a raise or giving them the tools they need to work with a disability. If the employer doesn't respond in a way that makes things right for my client, I sometimes have to go to court to get justice for my client. This means that I have to write a complaint describing in detail what the employer did and why it violates the law. I file that complaint with a court, and I then have to work to prepare to prove to a judge and jury that what the employer did to my client violates the law, and that the law requires the employer to make things right for my client. That process can be very complicated, and it can take months or even years before we find out whether we won a case.

Julia Taylor Brandus

What skills are the most important for you to know to do your job?

For starters, civil rights lawyers have to have a strong sense of justice and a clear understanding of the laws that protect clients. Being a civil rights lawyer involves a lot of reading and writing. We have to read all of the important decisions that the Supreme Court and other courts publish, and we have to understand how those decisions affect our clients. We also have to be good writers and storytellers. I have to tell my client's story and convince others that what an employer did violated the law.

What do you like best about your job?

In general, I like people, so I like getting to know my clients and feeling that I have made a difference in their lives by helping them seek justice. My clients are strong, hard-working people, and many of them suffer terribly because of what their employers did to them. Just knowing them and telling their stories has made me a better person.

What did you study in college, and where did you go?

I went to college at the University of Southern California, where I studied music and biology. (I wanted to be a professional violinist, and my dad wanted me to be a doctor.) I was also interested in other things, including international politics, so I took as many classes in that area as I could.

What do you know now that you wish you had known at age ten?

I realize now how hard my parents worked!

What is the one best piece of advice you have for young girls who will be going to high school, college, and joining the workforce in the next decade or so?

Be yourself, and be proud of who you are. Things have probably changed a lot since I grew up, but somewhere along the way, someone might tell you that you will be better at what you do or more likable if you look or speak or act a certain way. I see messages like this directed at girls and women far too often, even today.

For example, when I was a new lawyer, some people told me that I didn't sound tough enough, and that I needed to speak in a more aggressive tone and act like I was ready to fight with attorneys who were my opponents. I tried that for a while, but then I started to see that the lawyers I admired the most were the people who were decent, kind, and respectful, and they were often the best lawyers too. I enjoyed my job much more and developed better relationships with people when I learned that it's okay to just be who I am.

Is there a quote, an inspirational thought, or anything like that that motivates you each day?

I have a magnet in my kitchen that has a quote from Eleanor Roosevelt: "Use privilege to sow justice." I don't think Ms. Roosevelt used the term "privilege" to refer to skin color or to make anyone feel guilty about being fortunate, but I do think she meant that each of us has a responsibility to use whatever talents or skills we have to make the world a better place for everyone.

Can you tell me about a professional or personal setback you had, how you overcame it, and what you learned from it?

I wanted to be a professional violinist, and I worked very hard toward that goal. When I was fifteen, I first started to notice a problem with my left hand (the one that places fingers on the strings) in which I would feel sharp pain and my fingers would stiffen and lock up. It happened infrequently at first, but later, when I was playing professionally, it happened more often, sometimes during important performances. I had to give up a career doing something I loved. I overcame that setback by looking at it as an opportunity to pursue other academic interests. Those other interests brought me to Washington, D.C., which I now call home, and the career that I now enjoy. I learned that when one door closes, one has only to look for the others that are open.

> "Each of us has a responsibility to use whatever talents or skills we have to make the world a better place for everyone."
>
> —Subhashini Bollini

now

with Dad and Uncle

THEN

Susan Friedlander Earman

General District Court Judge

📍 Fairfax County, Virginia

Every citizen is entitled to fair and equal treatment under the law.

Hello, Your Honor! You are a District Court Judge. What is a judge, and what do you do?

A judge presides over trials. Either a bench trial (where the judge decides the case) or a jury trial (a jury gets to decide the case). The elevated desk a judge uses is called a bench.

As a judge I preside over traffic, criminal, and civil proceedings. I must maintain order and decide what evidence is appropriate. I don't preside over jury trials, but a judge in a jury trial gives the jury instructions about the law that apply to the case and the standards the jury must use in deciding the case. As a bench trial judge, I get to determine the facts and decide the case. In a criminal case I decide the sentence of convicted criminal defendants, such as what fines, jail time, and other conditions will be imposed.

There is a General District Court in each city and county in Virginia. The General District Court handles traffic violations, hears minor criminal cases known as misdemeanors, and conducts preliminary hearings for more serious criminal cases called felonies.

General District Courts have exclusive authority to hear civil cases with claims of $4,500 or less and share authority with the circuit courts to hear cases with claims between $4,500 and $25,000, and up to $50,000 in civil cases for personal injury and wrongful death. Examples of civil cases are landlord and tenant disputes, contract disputes such as construction or employment contracts and suits in debt, such as a credit card debt that went unpaid.

What skills are the most important for a judge to know?

A judge must be a good listener and be patient with the public. Most people in Virginia, if they come to court, will be in the General District Court. As a judge you need to understand how nervous they may feel or scared and help them know that the process will be fair and equitable. Of course, a judge must know and understand the law and how to apply it. Critical thinking is imperative, but compassion is needed as well.

What do you like best about being a judge?

I love interacting with the public. Every person has a story on how they are here in this world and why they are appearing in court. I make decisions with ease after hearing the evidence and explain my rulings. As a General District Court judge I can also require people to get help with substance abuse, or mental health assessments. Many times, people steal or trespass because they have no stability, no home, no job, and have addictive behaviors. I am proud that Fairfax County has programs to help people not commit the same types of crimes repeatedly. Providing tools for people to help themselves creates success.

A judge presiding over civil cases allows a person to have their day in court and say what they need to say within the parameters of judicial order. This public service makes me grateful to have such an important role for the citizens of Virginia.

What did you study in college, and where did you go?

I attended the University of Virginia and majored in mathematics. I received my law degree at George Mason University, now Antonin Scalia Law School.

What do you know now that you wish you had known at age ten?

The choices I made helped prepare me for this important role. I was an awkward, shy girl. I was afraid to speak in public and would cry if I had to give an oral report. I was so self-conscious and always felt like an outsider. I would tell my ten-year-old self that anything was possible and to enjoy my school life, to not to be so anxious, and to take risks. And I would remind myself to learn from mistakes and that failures only make you a better person. Maybe I would be able to convince my ten-year-old self what the "small stuff" was and tell myself, "Don't sweat the small stuff!"

What is the one best piece of advice you have for young girls who will be going to high school, college, and joining the workforce in the next decade or so?

I would suggest that they work hard and take diverse courses. Diversity in learning may allow them to find out what else may be of interest. Each job you take, even if it isn't your passion, will teach you something of value or you'll meet a person to help you in your future. I loved to work, and every time, I met someone of importance or learned something new. One of my favorite jobs was working at the McDonalds in McLean, Virginia, when I was in high school, and I learned that people worked hard to support their loved ones and that they took pride in tasks that some would find routine.

"I would tell my ten-year-old self that anything was possible and to enjoy my school life and not to be so anxious."

—Judge Susan Friedlander Earman

Stacey Kincaid

Sheriff

📍 **Fairfax County, Virginia**

Helping to enforce the law and keep citizens safe!

Hello! You are a sheriff. What does a sheriff do?

I am a Constitutional Law Enforcement Officer elected by the citizens of Fairfax County, the City of Fairfax, and the Towns of Herndon and Vienna, Virginia. I lead an agency of over five hundred dedicated men and women who make us the best sheriff's office in Virginia. We are responsible for operating the Adult Detention Center; providing security for the courthouse, judges, and many thousands of visitors every day; and serving civil documents on behalf of the courts.

As sheriff, I am responsible for ensuring my staff are well trained and have the knowledge, skills, and abilities to carry out our responsibilities effectively and efficiently.

What skills are the most important for someone in your role to know?

As a leader, it is important that people know I am human, have made mistakes, and believe in second chances. I am firm but fair and hold people accountable. I believe effective communication is one of the most important skills in getting the message across to avoid misunderstandings. Communication is something that can make or break an agency. It is also one of the skills that goes hand in hand with being a good listener. It is helpful for driving change, solving problems, motivating staff, and getting things done.

I expect a lot from my staff, and they in turn should expect a lot from me because I work for them. I ask lots of questions and let my staff know that it is okay to fail. It is a way for them to learn, develop, and grow, both personally and professionally. I am understanding, passionate about the work I do, and care about my people. I am patient, strategic and look at things from a global perspective. I like to see the big picture.

What do you like best about being a sheriff?

I like having the opportunity to meet new people and learn from them. I like being able to help people overcome difficulties, to succeed where others had given up on them. I fight for the underdog and try to right the wrongs. I can give people the tools they need to make their lives better, and they in turn, can do the same for others. I love having the ability to help others, to work with families and to make a difference. The best part about being the sheriff is having the opportunity to be a role model.

What did you study in college, and where did you go?

I went to Frostburg State University in Maryland and majored in political science with a concentration in criminal justice.

What do you know now that you wish you had known at age ten?

At ten years old, I thought I was going to be a teacher, a lawyer, or a famous actress. Although none of these careers came to fruition, I did star in six episodes of the MSNBC *Lock Up Fairfax* series and played Sheriff Stacey Kincaid!

What is the one best piece of advice you have for young girls who will be going to high school, college, and joining the workforce in the next decade or so?

Every day of your life, you have the opportunity to learn, grow, and make choices. Always remember, every choice you make has consequences, whether good or bad. Never stop believing in yourself and knowing you can be anything you want to be. Be kind to others. Use good judgment and do the right thing, even if you think no one is watching.

Contribute to your community in the most productive way that you are able. To be a good citizen is part of having good character. It means that you are trustworthy, respectful, and responsible. You have integrity.

Is there a quote, an inspirational thought, or anything like that that motivates you each day?

"Be the change you wish to see in the world." —Mahatma Gandhi

Is there anything you would like to add that we are not asking here?

I am proud to be the first woman to lead the Fairfax County Sheriff's Office in our 279-year history. When I was first elected in 2013, I was not new to the agency. I was a college intern for the Sheriff's Office providing one-on-one counseling to inmates and working in the Inmate Programs office. That internship led me to apply for a position as a Deputy Sheriff. A month after I graduated, I was employed as a Deputy Sheriff. Over the years, I worked my way up to the rank of Captain before running for office. I ran for Sheriff because I wanted to be an agent of change and make this agency a leader in both the law enforcement community and the Fairfax County community at large. I am happy to say that we are! We have launched several innovative programs and are recognized nationally for the work we do regarding mental illness, substance use disorders, and re-entry programs inside the Adult Detention Center and out in the community. We are an essential part of the Fairfax County public safety family. And I am very proud of the diverse group of professional men and women who work for the Sheriff's Office. Every action we take—or don't take—affects our ability to carry out our mission and influences our reputation in the communities we serve.

> "Use good judgment and do the right thing, even if you think no one is watching."
>
> —Stacey Kincaid

Marketing

Kathryne Reeves

Chief Marketing Officer,
Illumina, Inc.

📍 **San Diego, California**

> The science and art of identifying an audience—a market—for a product or service.

**Hello, Ms. Reeves! You are the chief marketing officer at Il-
lumina. Please tell us what Illumina is, and about your job
as a chief marketing officer.**

As the chief marketing officer, I'm the one person, our CEO
(chief executive officer), our company, our shareholders, and
our customers count on to deliver the marketing strategy and
execution for the company. At Illumina, we create very so-
phisticated biotechnology devices that help scientists and researchers and hospital systems and doctors find information
about our genetics. We make devices that make doing something called "genomic sequencing" very simple and inexpen-
sive. My job is to market those products to all of our prospec-
tive customers around the world. That can be everything from
deciding what features the product has, to how the product
works, and working with our engineers to say, "Hey, our customers would really love it if our products did this." Or, "Our
customers would really love it if our product costs this much
money." So, doing all kinds of research with our customers.

Then I also do things that are super fun. I make adver-
tisements and videos and all kinds of things that promote
the product to our potential customers globally. That is such
a huge responsibility because we really believe that if more
and more scientists and researchers use our products, it'll help
them discover exciting new things about human biology that
have never been known before. So that's the really most awe-
some part of my job.

You mentioned genomic sequencing. What is that?

So there's something called DNA. DNA is essentially the
roadmap of our biology. It explains who we are and our lineage. Every person born, every plant that grows, every creature

that crawls the earth or swims in the sea came from parents or from an egg. That DNA that they inherited from their lineage gives vital information about how that specific person functions. If we can find out what that DNA says, then it allows us to do some pretty extraordinary things in the field of medicine and in the field of climate change, or in the fields of pathogen surveillance. So maybe I'll use the simpler word, tracking down the kinds of viruses that can kill us, like COVID-19. So that's really what our products let scientists do in their labs, and it's actually really cool stuff.

Our technology allows researchers and clinicians and lots of very smart people to understand what this DNA is doing in living organisms and how that makes them different in terms of their characteristics. This brings us closer to solving some major diseases, too, major diseases like cancer. I must say there's even emerging research that shows that many common diseases like heart disease have very strong indications from variations inherited. Our real goal is to make a disease not something that you can inherit. That we could detect disease, and that we could help create medicines and therapeutics that are tailored to each and every person to help resolve their illness without really bad drugs like chemotherapy.

Wow! What skills are the most important for you to know to do your job?

One is to be very curious. The very best marketers are very, very curious. They spend a lot of time trying to figure out what it is that makes our customers happy and the things that would make them even happier. They really enjoy investigating and understanding what makes that happen. If you were to talk to a really great marketer, they're super curious. They're the type of person you would meet and then they would ask you fifteen thousand questions and you'd probably get exhausted because you're like, "Why are you asking me so many questions?" But that's the type of person that a marketer is. So it's funny, you're very curious, obviously, to be writing a book at such a young age and you are asking people lots of questions so maybe, who knows, in your future you might want to be someone in marketing.

Have you ever picked up your Apple phone or a very cool coloring book—my daughter loved really cool coloring books—and you wondered, "How did they know I would like to have my phone work this way, or for it to look like this or come in so many cool colors?" It's because some marketers spent thousands of hours asking customers questions like, "Well, what are your favorite colors? And what would you like to see in a coloring book, what types of things would you like to color?" If you're the kind of person who's just super curious and asks those questions and does a really good job listening, really, really listening, you would make a great marketer. Another skill that's really great in excellent marketers is something called empathy. Do you know what the word empathy means?

Yes. That's what they teach in school.

Maybe a simple way to think about empathy is some people have kind of an intuition or a feeling inside of their heart and they can sense whether someone's happy or sad or whether someone wants to be cheered up or whether someone's really excited and wants to have a party or maybe they're a little down and depressed. They can sense that without even knowing because they just are really good at picking up on other people's vibes or other people's energy. If you're a really good marketer, you can sense when, "We need to improve our situation. Our customers really hate this thing about our product, or they really love this thing about our product, and I need to take this information to our engineers, or I need to take this information to our salespeople and I need to make sure we fix it."

So if you're that kind of person who likes to pick up on the energy of other people and can put yourself in other people's shoes and really understand what makes them tick, that is an excellent marketer. I really love it when we're sitting around in a business meeting and we're making a decision, and one of the marketers on my team will say something like, "I think we're talking about everybody but the customer. Here's what I learned, here's what customers are saying, and I want us to pay attention." That is a super empathetic person. Then the last best skill you will ever find in a marketer is a team player. That's someone who has super strong opinions and really has strengthened their convictions. That's kind of a big word. But they're real believers, they're passionate, but they also like to win with a team. They like being together with other people. They like talking to other people. They don't like being alone. So those are the three things I really, over the years, have seen consistently be the case with great marketers. They're curious, they're empathetic, and they like being with other people.

What did you study in school, and where did you go?
I went to Stanford University in Palo Alto, California. I studied civil engineering (civil engineers are involved with the design and construction of things like buildings, bridges, roads, etc.). Then I went to the Harvard Graduate School of Business and obtained a master's degree in business in 1995.

What do you know now that you wish you had known at age ten?

Really nothing. I know that we're supposed to be kind to our younger selves and give advice, but I think the best thing about being ten is just being ten and going through life and experiencing things and not being under the pressure to get everything right. So I think just be ten, go through what it's like to be ten: sleepovers, going to the movies, playing sports, playing outside, playing video games.

What is one of the best pieces of advice that you have for young girls who will be going to high school, college, and joining the workforce in the next decade or so?

I think I like people that have two characteristics. I like people who are super smart and super nice. So if you've got a combination of being a real go-getter, super smart, can handle yourself in any situation, but also really like being with people, being a great team member, that's an unbeatable combination.

I also think that pursuing your studies and being very focused on getting good grades is also very, very important, and cannot be underestimated.

Can you tell me about a professional or a personal setback you had and how you overcame it and what you learned from it?

Oh, sure. There've been so many. First of all, I think accepting highs and lows, wins and losses is very important. How you lose is more important than how you win. So people who are poor sports and sorry losers I think are the worst kinds of people. So even if you battle very, very hard and you lose a game, I've always insisted my children shake the hand of their opponent and be a good sport. It's very, very important. That's true in business. So I've been in very tough competitions where I put a great proposal together and sold my heart out and lost the business. Invariably, customers will say we've actually won business back because of how we handled ourselves when we lost. That really does define who you are. So I think having high character in both victory and defeat is very, very important, and always conducting yourself with a high character. So I don't have a lot of patience for cheaters and liars and people who badmouth their competition.

Is there anything you would like to add that we're not asking you here?

Well, I think that there's a superpower to being a girl that you should just absolutely love about yourself. I think our country and our culture can sometimes rush girls into being women. I think there's just something super cool and fabulous about being a girl. Sometimes you get teased for being a girl or sometimes you might get bullied, but I think being a girl, it's like when I look back in my life, some of my happiest, happiest times were playing with my friends, being outside, and just being a girl. So it's just super cool. It's super special. I really think that just cherish these years and enjoy your years as a girl, because adolescence will be here soon enough.

> "Having high character in both victory and defeat is very, very important, and always conducting yourself with a high character."
>
> —Kathryne Reeves

Media, Arts, and Entertainment

now

THEN

Emily Greenspan

Owner, Tag-Arts, and Art Consultant

📍 **Beverly Hills, California**

Art can make a home or place of business more beautiful, more comfortable, and more inviting.

Hello! You are the owner of Tag-Arts and are an art consultant. What is Tag-Arts, and what does an art consultant do?

Tag-Arts is an art consulting firm I created back in 2007 that provides guidance and advice to people buying art for their homes and businesses. I help in the process of selecting paintings, photography, sculpture, and other forms of artwork for buyers and their collections, negotiate prices, supervise how and where the artwork should be installed or placed—basically manage everything for an art collector in order to develop a contemporary art collection. I also assist clients who want to sell art or "downsize" their collection. Additionally, I work with artists to strategize and offer guidance to those seeking advice with their careers.

What skills and knowledge does an art consultant need to have?

It is important to have very good "people" skills or social skills since I talk to various kinds of people all the time: artists, collectors, gallery owners, museum curators, etc. It is also important to read a lot and learn as much as possible from the people you meet in the art world. Education is key, and there are so many artists and so much to know about each artist's practice, process, and career. I attend multiple art fairs, galleries, museums; visit artists in their studios to see their work firsthand; and of course, search the internet as well. It helps to have a great memory, but most of all it's important to love what you do and have a true passion for it.

What do you like best about being an art consultant?

I love meeting talented artists all the time and seeing the tremendous amount of creativity that exists and how it is expressed so differently by so many remarkable groups of people. I also love working with various kinds of clients from all over the world and meeting their diverse needs and desires. Every project is unique, which makes each day fun, exciting, and challenging. I am also lucky that I get to travel for work sometimes to art fairs, to visit clients, and to meet new artists, which is always so enjoyable! Being in different places is so inspiring and exhilarating.

What did you study in college, and where did you go?

I graduated from Washington University in St. Louis, MO, with a bachelor of arts in French and a double minor in art history and English literature.

What do you know now that you wish you had known at age ten?

I don't need to learn calculus!

What is the one best piece of advice you have for girls who will be going to high school, college, and joining the workforce in the next decade or so?

Behind every successful woman is…herself!

Is there a quote, an inspirational thought, or anything like that that motivates you each day?

I read an inspirational quote every day…. Here is what I read this morning: "I am not a product of my circumstances. I am a product of my decisions."

Is there anything you would like to add that we are not asking here?

My personal advice: don't be afraid to change jobs or classes or directions in life. What I thought I wanted to do or be is not what I am doing now, but I am so glad for the journey. All my experiences have taught me to take my knowledge from all my various encounters and use them how I see fit. Previously, I worked as an editor at a magazine, in the buying office for a well-known clothing label, as a salesperson in my father's antiques business…. I have been lucky to have had wonderful teachers and mentors along the way and have been able to take skills and lessons from each and apply them to how I conduct myself and my business today.

> "I am not a product of my circumstances. I am a product of my decisions."
>
> —Emily Greenspan

Eun Sun Kim

Music Director, San Francisco Opera

📍 **San Francisco, California**

> A musical performance by an ensemble must be shaped over time, from rehearsal to performance.

Hello! You are the music director of the San Francisco Opera. What does a music director do? Please tell me about your job.

My job has two main parts. The first involves collaborating with many different groups of people to make music. As a conductor, I lead the orchestra in the pit as well as the chorus and solo singers on stage. I also work with stage directors, who direct the action the audience sees, and stage managers, who keep everything running smoothly backstage during the show. The second part of my job as music director is administrative leadership, from big decisions like which shows we should perform each season and which artists should sing with us, to day-to-day work like listening to a recording and deciding whether it's a good representation of our sound and can be approved for streaming.

What skills are the most important for you to know to do your job?

As a music director, you need to be quite patient and also have the courage to act when the time is right. You need to be very comfortable with accountability, since you are the musical CEO of your company—you are responsible for the artistic product your company puts out. Most importantly, you must have integrity and a deep belief that you can connect people with music.

What do you like best about your job?

Music speaks to everyone differently; it can be inspiring and transformative, and it's a very individual experience that many people can have at the same moment. Helping people experience that connection to music through my job makes me very happy.

What did you study in college, and where did you go?

I studied composition, which is writing new music, and orchestral conducting at Yonsei University in Seoul, South Korea. I then moved to Germany, where I earned my doctorate in orchestral conducting from the University of Music in Stuttgart.

What do you know now that you wish you had known at age ten?

I enjoyed every age of my life as it was, actually; I had just the right information for ten-year-old me! I believe there is always a right moment to learn certain things about life, which keeps me excited about what I might learn today or tomorrow.

What is the one best piece of advice you have for young girls who will be going to high school, college, and joining the workforce in the next decade or so?

Tackle the task in front of you with 100 percent of your energy, whether that's learning at school, practicing a hobby, or working at a company. This focus makes it much easier to stay present in the moment and enjoy your life as it happens each day!

Is there a quote, an inspirational thought, or anything like that that motivates you each day?

There are so many! Here are two that have guided me most. First, "You say what you mean, and you mean what you say." I highly recommend living with integrity in this way. Second, Thomas Aquinas said, "If the highest aim of a captain were to preserve his ship, he would keep it in port forever." This quote reminds me that a certain amount of risk-taking is a part of fulfilling our life's goals—we are meant to set sail!

Can you tell me about a professional or personal setback you had, how you overcame it, and what you learned from it?

I learn new things every day, from every experience, and I try not to view those as setbacks. I've learned that it's actually a crucial part of growth to make mistakes along the way. Adapting in order to not repeat a mistake is when you learn and get better!

Is there anything you would like to add that we are not asking here?

The world is big and you never know how your life will evolve in the future. I was born and grew up in Asia, studied and worked in Europe, and now I have started a new life in North America. Keep an open mind and an eye out for opportunities that intrigue you—I am excited for all of you!

"You say what you mean, and you mean what you say."

—Eun Sun Kim

now

Photo by Michael Lavine

THEN

Jill Hennessy

Actor, Singer, Songwriter

📍 **New York, New York**

Jill is currently starring in Fox's *Accused* and Showtime's *City on a Hill*. She previously spent many years on NBC's *Law & Order*, and *Crossing Jordan*. She has also been in more than thirty movies and performed on Broadway.

> A life of performing. On stage, on camera. Writing songs, singing!

Hello, Jill! You're an actor. What's that like? Tell me about your job.

When you're actually acting, the feelings you experience range from extreme joy, terror, and self-discovery, to a wonderful sense of freedom, connection, and acknowledgement. Unfortunately, an actor spends the majority of their time just looking for work, and if you're lucky enough to find some, you need to figure out how to support yourself and/or your family with a job that may require a lot of travel, little job security, etc. But the possibility of telling someone's story, creating something from your experience, or creating something out of thin air is tremendously exciting! Every role gives the opportunity to do research and educate yourself about historical figures (Jackie Kennedy was such a joy to study and portray!), different cultures, issues, and other points of view you might not have been aware of.

What skills are the most important for you to know to be a good actor?

I would say that the most important skill for being a good actor (and maybe a good person as well) is to be a good listener. The more one really listens to others and their respective stories and paths, the more able you'll be to relate to them and tell their stories…as well as your own!

What do you like best about being an actor?

Wow! Acting allows me to feel like a kid on Halloween where I can be anyone, look different, dress in costumes and play with fascinating people (and there's even candy available almost all of the time on sets!). I guess I just feel really happy and alive when I'm working with other artists, as though we're just a bunch of kids on a playground. I also love giving voice to stories that are meaningful and need to be told.

What did you study in college, and where did you go?

Although I highly recommend college to all, that wasn't really a financially viable choice for me. Instead, I found work as a casting assistant (an invaluable experience for actors), waitress, bartender, and street musician to pay for various acting classes at different studios in Toronto and New York.

What do you know now that you wish you had known at age ten?

I guess I wish I had known that fear doesn't have to be an obstacle or a "stop sign," that you can still try something though it might seem terrifying. And that I was, indeed, "good enough." Some of life's greatest accomplishments are achieved when moving through one's own fear. Fear of what others think about you is an especially deceptive illusion.

What is the one best piece of advice you have for young girls who will be going to high school, college, and joining the workforce in the next decade or so?

It's pretty tough coming up with just one answer for this.... Some simple advice I would give is to always look people in the eye when meeting or dealing with them; see their humanity. Something as seemingly obvious as looking someone in the eye and connecting with them helps a great deal not only in school, but in future workplaces and relationships. No matter what you look like, sound like, however "different" you may feel you are, only you have your own history, unique gifts, and abilities. You not only deserve to be in the room, they would be lucky to have you. Also, try everything! You might discover your true passion or talent. And if something doesn't work out, change direction and keep moving to something else. It's ok to say no. But keep on moving. You don't have to know exactly what you will want to pursue in life by high school or college; follow your instincts, find your passion and talents.

Is there a quote, an inspirational thought, or anything like that that motivates you each day?

I often think about the Eleanor Roosevelt quote: "No one can make you feel inferior without your consent." Also, Maya Angelou hits me pretty profoundly with her quote: "There is no greater agony than bearing an untold story inside you." In fact, I highly recommend looking at everything Maya Angelou has written.

Tell me about a setback you've had in life, and what you learned from it.

I've had a number of moments in my life where I've experienced situations of loss and crisis that left me struggling to even breathe. I started writing about these experiences as a form of therapy, and much of the content became stories, songs, two albums and then led to live musical performances in the U.S., Canada, and Europe. Through playing my own songs, telling my own stories, and making my own albums, I've met so many people with similar experiences and have loved getting the chance to share and connect with them.

> **"Always look people in the eye when meeting or dealing with them."**
>
> —Jill Hennessy

now

THEN

Margaret Wallace

Entrepreneur, Gaming and Media Professional, Co-Founder of Playmatics (video gaming); Professor, Boston University

Boston, Massachusetts

There are some 2.2 billion video gamers in the world today![7]

Girl to BOSS!

Hello! You are the co-founder of Playmatics. What is that, and what do you do? Please tell me about your job.

I'm a video game developer and have been for much of my adult life. My company, Playmatics, which I founded back in 2009, was formed to focus on creating innovative games that everyone can play. I came up with the name "Playmatics" from a desire to find a way to combine the concept of "play" with "mathematics," because the creation of video games involves art, math, design, and a little bit of magic. Making a successful video game is one of the hardest things to accomplish—even the simplest game can be complex to make from a "fun" and also a moment-to-moment interaction standpoint. Games are not passive experiences, and players understandably have very high expectations.

To make these games over the years, I've raised money, negotiated deals, hired production teams, designed gameplay, and have led distribution and promotion efforts. When I started working in the games industry, it was very niche. Now the games industry is one of the hottest sectors around. For example, some estimates indicate that there are 3.4 billion gamers worldwide and that games are probably the most pervasive form of entertainment worldwide.

What skills are the most important for you to know to do your job?

Entrepreneurs wear many hats. Sometimes this involves business negotiation, product design, and speaking at conferences. My job is never boring because every day is filled with variety.

To make a successful video game, it's important for the creator to be able to iterate (change) quickly on concepts. The last thing a game developer wants to do is spend too much

185

time on a game that will not appeal to players. The hours can be long, but I derive enormous satisfaction from being able to work on things that are innovative and meaningful to me as a founder and as a creator.

Games are used for all sorts of things these days—beyond entertainment—so it's important to anticipate trends and figure out where games are going in light of new platforms, player preferences, and technological innovation. I am required to play games all the time and stay up to date in terms of what's happening in the world of movies, sports, music, even science and healthcare.

What do you like best about being a videogame designer?

I really enjoy thinking through game design challenges and also coming up with characters for my games. I also really enjoy the technical aspect of game development—thinking through with my engineers how to solve certain problems or make sure everything is working smoothly from a user experience standpoint. I am generally fascinated by technology and the notion of developing games that potentially thousands of people will play.

What did you study in college, and where did you go?

For my undergraduate studies, I was a student at Boston University (BU). I studied communication research and focused my studies on the cultural impact of everyday technologies. BU was a great environment because I was given the freedom to pursue my academic interests. At college, I made lifelong friends and had a chance to be a research assistant for one of my professors, who was an inspiration.

After BU, I was a graduate student at the University of Massachusetts/Amherst (UMass) and continued my studies in communication research. At UMass, I graduated with a master's degree and wrote my thesis on women-led punk rock bands that were popular during that time.

Given my current career, I probably would have been well served taking a couple of computer programming classes. However, it's never too late, and I take programming classes every now and then to help me be a better game developer.

What do you know now that you wish you had known at age ten?

Every day is a chance to do or experience something amazing, maybe even transformative.

What is the one best piece of advice you have for young girls who will be going to high school, college, and joining the workforce in the next decade or so?

Never let anyone tell you that you don't belong. Always stay curious and adaptive to changes in the world and in your chosen professional field. Every company is increasingly becoming a data-centered company, so it's important to have a good grasp of how to read, manipulate, and visualize data for making informed decisions.

Can you tell me about a professional or personal setback you had, how you overcame it, and what you learned from it?

The biggest challenge I've encountered professionally is being a woman working in the tech and games industries and the ongoing bias that women experience every day in big and small ways. As much as it's important to focus on the positive aspects of being a game developer, it's equally important to remember that progress is slow and not always steady in terms of embracing diversity, equity, and inclusion. I have learned that grit and staying focused help a lot. I also learned how important it is to take ownership of your own narrative, to define who you are and (as much as possible) not let people project their expectations of who they assume you are onto you.

Is there a quote, an inspirational thought, or anything like that that motivates you each day?

"When you change the way you look at things, the things you look at change."—Max Planck

Is there anything you would like to add that we are not asking here?

I like to joke that "showing up" is a major ingredient for success. I can't begin to say how many amazing people I've met and the benefits I've gained just by putting myself out there, whether attending events, speaking at conferences, and generally being open to exploring new opportunities. It's great to network, even if it's a bit outside one's comfort zone, because scheduled meetings and chance encounters alike can lead to life-changing experiences. If I had not bothered and stayed home—I would have missed out on so much.

> **"Never let anyone tell you that you don't belong."**
>
> —Margaret Wallace

Medicine and Healthcare

now

THEN

Dr. Rina Bansal, MD, MBA

President, Inova Alexandria Hospital

📍 **Alexandria, Virginia**

Only 37 percent of America's doctors are women.[8] More doctors are needed!

Hello, Doctor! You are the President of Inova Alexandria Hospital. Can you tell me about Inova Alexandria Hospital, and what a hospital president does?

Inova Alexandria Hospital is a community hospital, which means that we have the privilege of taking care of each and every person in the community who is feeling sick or has an illness. This could be someone who hurt their arm and comes to the emergency room for an X-ray, someone who has appendicitis and needs surgery or someone who has a problem with their heart and needs to be admitted to the hospital. We also deliver babies and take care of the very small babies in our Neonatal Intensive Care Unit.

As the president of the hospital, my role is to make sure that everything in the hospital is running smoothly, from the floors being clean to the staff taking exceptional care of their patients. My job is to care for my team members, make sure they are supported, and love coming to work, so that in turn, they can take care of the community.

What skills are the most important for someone in your role to know?

As a leader, intelligence and subject matter expertise/knowledge are foundational elements. However, what makes one a good leader are the qualities that define a good person, a mentor/coach, and a role model. Below are the qualities that I aspire to in my journey to be a good leader and lead my team to greater success.

1) Ability to Listen: listening with an open mind and heart

2) Dedication: dedication to serve your team members, patients, and community
3) Courage: courage to make difficult decisions and to lead with calm during tough times
4) Empathy: as a good leader, you must be able to put yourself in others' shoes and understand and share their feelings
5) Humility: humility to admit that you don't know everything and that sometimes you also may make mistakes

What do you like best about your role?

I truly love being able to take care of people, be it my team members or our patients. I also feel that this role makes me use every part of my brain, ranging from medical issues to relationship-building to leadership to finances. It is fun, challenging, and never boring.

What did you study in school, and where did you go?

I moved from India to Overland Park, Kansas, in 1987 when I was fourteen years old. I attended Shawnee Mission Northwest High School and subsequently graduated from University of Kansas with a BA in biology and BS in genetics. After college, I was fortunate to attend McGill University in Montreal, Canada. There I pursued a combined degree in medicine as well as a master's in business administration (MBA). It was a very busy five years, but I learned so much and got to live in a really cool French-speaking city. Subsequently, I completed a residency in internal medicine at University of California, San Francisco, one of the top internal medicine programs in the country.

What do you know now that you wish you had known at age ten?

At the age of ten, I was a driven, idealistic, and responsible child but a free spirit. I was very independent, not afraid of most things. I loved learning and school, played sports, did arts and crafts. Honestly, I can't think of anything I wish I had known back then. I wish kids today were less exposed to the world and had more time to grow up innocent.

What is the one best piece of advice you have for young girls who will be going to high school, college, and joining the workforce in the next decade or so?

Follow your passion, work hard, and never give up. There were many points in my life where I had to make tough decisions, such as when I decided to come back to the United States for college on my own or when I could not get into medical school because I was not a U.S. citizen and did not have enough money to go to a private medical school. I kept trying and working hard and eventually got into a program that was an innovative combined degree program that set me up for success later in life.

Is there a quote, an inspirational thought, or anything like that that motivates you each day?

"You must be the change you wish to see in the world."
—Mahatma Gandhi

I admire Mahatma Gandhi, who led a successful non-violent resistance campaign to end British rule in India, for many reasons. However, his quote above resonates the most with me. To me, it signifies that change comes from within oneself. This is especially important as a leader in creating the right organizational culture that aligns with the company's mission, vision, and values to achieve outcomes and succeed.

Is there anything you would like to add that we are not asking here?

I am honored to be the president of Inova Alexandria Hospital and fortunate to be able to serve humanity. Although, as a woman, you may come across some unique challenges, always remember that there is nothing that should hold you back. I see being a female leader as an asset and not a weakness. Do not let others define you; redefine the world around you.

> **"Always remember that there is nothing that should hold you back."**
>
> —Dr. Rina Bansal

now

THEN

Jean Braden

Nurse Practitioner,
The Children's Clinic

📍 Billings, Montana

More than two million new nurses
will be needed by 2031, and many
more in the years after that.[9]

Hello! You are a nurse practitioner. Please tell me about your job.

I work in a pediatric office delivering care to teenagers and young adults. I worked in a hospital as a registered nurse for many years and then went back to school to advance my degree and become a nurse practitioner.

What skills are the most important for you to know to do your job?

I think anyone in the healthcare profession must greet every single day with the fortitude to do their job with excellence. I work with a parents' most prized possession: their children. There is really no room for error. Every day I must do my job to the best of my ability. I must be a good listener so I don't miss a subtle symptom that may help me make a correct diagnosis. I must be respectful and approach every patient and parent knowing that they may forget what I SAY but how I make them FEEL could stay with them for a lifetime.

What do you like best about your job?

I love getting to touch a life in a very personal way, every single day. I not only get to have a job that is rewarding intellectually, but every day the personal interactions I have with families "fills me up."

What did you study in college, and where did you go?

I studied nursing at Montana State University in Bozeman, Montana, becoming a registered nurse in 1981. It was a five-hour drive from my hometown and located in the mountains of one of Montana's most beautiful areas. I had never lived outside of my tiny town of 3,500 people, so it was a very exciting time for me. I later attended UCLA (University of

California, Los Angeles) and was certified to be a nurse practitioner in 1986.

What do you know now that you wish you had known at age ten?

That I am enough. I am smart enough, creative enough, and will go on to have a very rewarding and joyful life. I was a worrier and afraid of making mistakes. I wish that ten-year-old girl had more self-confidence and less fear.

What is the one best piece of advice you have for young girls who will be going to high school, college, and joining the workforce in the next decade or so?

Really think about what you have an interest in and a passion for. When you find that passion, your job will never be "work." I think my girls (Megan and Hannah) experienced this as they were growing up. My job never seemed to them like it was "work" for me. So, they both chose the nursing profession as well.

Is there a quote, an inspirational thought, or anything like that that motivates you each day?

Well, I have many. "It's good to have money and the things money can buy, but it's good, too, to check up once in a while and make sure that you haven't lost the things money can't buy..." —George Horace Lorimer

Can you tell me about a professional or personal setback you had, how you overcame it, and what you learned from it?

In 2008, I lost my husband—the father of my daughters Hannah and Megan—very unexpectedly. He was only fifty-one. He was a wonderful, loving husband and father. We were devastated, but I decided at that moment that everything I did from that moment would be done with the health and wellness of my girls in mind. Life was hard, but my girls learned the importance of creating a village and surrounding yourself with people of true substance who help in times of trouble and give of themselves unconditionally. They have since created this in their own lives.

In that loss I learned that I was so much more capable than I ever dreamed. I learned how lucky I was to have experienced true love, if only for twenty-eight years. It has made me more appreciative and grateful and made me a more compassionate person. It created resilience in both myself and my girls. When bad things happen, we have three choices: we can let it define us, destroy us, or strengthen us. We worked through our loss while continuing with life, and this strengthened us. Living through our loss has allowed for us to be little beacons of light and hope for other families experiencing the same.

Is there anything you would like to add that we are not asking here?

I truly feel women are hardwired to be problem solvers, truth tellers, and when armed with self-confidence and a good education, they will save the world! My wish for you is that you have the self-confidence to believe you can do anything you set your mind to, that you approach life with joy and a sense of community, never missing an opportunity to brighten someone's life in even the smallest of ways. Be a problem solver!

"Be a problem solver!"

—Jean Braden

now

THEN

Dr. Sandy Ibrahim

Primary Care Physician, Medical Director, Inova 360° Concierge Medicine

📍 Fairfax, Virginia

"Cure sometimes, treat often, and comfort always."
—Hippocrates

Hello, Doctor! You are a primary care physician. What is that, and what do you do?

Inova 360° is a primary care medical program. I am a full-time family doctor and I am also the director of the program. I am the boss of twelve other primary care doctors who care for over four thousand patients. We also have about four hundred clients from around the world who are top executives with their companies or organizations. Each spends a day in our offices for a comprehensive physical exam.

What skills are the most important for a doctor to know?

Doctors must obviously have a great command of the biological sciences. In addition to this, I think that doctors must also have a gift in being able to communicate well and to have empathy. These are two skills that I use each day with every patient. It is one thing to know the science, but you must also communicate that science in an effective way. Empathy is important because sometimes we have to deliver difficult news to a beloved patient. It helps to be resilient.

What do you like best about being a doctor?

I absolutely love growing with my patients. Some of my patients have been under my care for over fifteen years now. We have celebrated their personal and professional milestones, been through illnesses and recovery and their wellness journey together, and I feel as if they are a part of my family.

What did you study in college, and where did you go?

Becoming a doctor is not easy. We have to make it through four years of college, four years of medical school, and in my field, family medicine, an additional three years of residency! It is a long journey to become a doctor. I have a bachelor's degree in microbiology from the University of Michigan in Ann Arbor. I have a medical degree from Wayne State University in Detroit, Michigan and I spent three years in residency training at Providence Hospital in Southfield, Michigan.

What do you know now that you didn't know when you were nine, ten, or eleven?

What I wish I knew at the age of ten is that the path of least resistance is what I should have focused on. When I was younger, it was always about the best schools, the most sports and school clubs, the longest resume, and the loudest voice in the room meant "success." I wish I would have spent more time enjoying each life event for its actual experience in the moment, rather than for what it would "potentially" bring to me in the future!

What is the one best piece of advice you have for young girls who will be going to high school, college, and entering the workforce in the next decade or so?

My advice is to surround yourselves with positive energy and positive people. Ignore the critics and naysayers. Make sure you are surrounded by people who will support your dreams and ambitions. Don't let anyone tell you that anything is unreachable, unlikely, or not meant to be. Also, don't be so hard on yourself! Life can be hard enough as it is. You need to be your most reliable cheerleader! Forge your path, especially if you are the first one to do it. I am the first doctor in my family!

Is there a quote, an inspirational thought, or anything like that that motivates you?

My motivation comes from my spirituality. I have many holy verses that could exemplify this, but in essence it is this: "After every storm, comes a rainbow."

Would you like to add anything else, Doctor?

Yes. I would like to add that the definition of success can be complex. It's not necessarily about financial success or status or fame. Success can mean many different things. For me, success is being the best version of myself that I can be and to be content with my best efforts. It is more important to me that I am happy at the end of my day from self-care, care for my loved ones, and how I make people feel after their encounters with me than about how many dollars are in the bank or how many letters are behind my name. I wear a lot of hats, as they say: mother, daughter, wife, sister, friend, neighbor, and doctor, and I hope I am doing all of them well when that particular hat is on my head!

> **"Ignore the critics and naysayers."**
>
> —Dr. Sandy Ibrahim

now

Photo by Lucas Passmore

THEN

Dr. Seema Yasmin

Epidemiologist, Stanford University; Professor, University of California, Los Angeles; Journalist

📍 Stanford and Los Angeles, California

"The aim of medicine is to prevent disease and prolong life; the ideal of medicine is to eliminate the need of a physician."
—Mayo Clinic Co-Founder Dr. William Mayo

Hi Doctor Yasmin! You're an epidemiologist—that's a big word!—at Stanford University, a "disease detective," and also a professor at UCLA. And a journalist. Please tell me about your jobs.

I'm really excited that I get to do all of the things that I'm passionate about! One of the things I do at Stanford is I track the spread of false information about health and science. I've been doing this for about four years at Stanford, but about ten years altogether. And I became worried about this, Julia, roughly ten years ago, when I left England to move to America. The job that I moved here for was as an officer in the Epidemic Intelligence Service (part of the Centers for Disease Control and the U.S. military). The EIS is a group of doctors and scientists that the federal government keeps on hand to act as medical sleuths. So, I'm a "disease detective!"

When there's an outbreak or a pandemic, they send us out to try and figure out what disease is spreading, and most importantly, what can we do to stop it from sickening or even killing more people. When I moved to America ten years ago for that job, I thought, oh, I'm going to be dealing with really strange, rare diseases. And there was some of that. But I was so shocked, Julia, that so many of the epidemics that I would get sent to deal with were diseases like measles and whooping cough and mumps, and as you know, we have vaccines that prevent those diseases! No one should be getting sick with those illnesses now.

But the reason that kids were becoming sick, *really sick*, from these preventable diseases, was because their parents were choosing not to vaccinate them. And it turned out that was because there was so much false information and hoaxes spreading about the vaccines, what was in them, what kind of scary health effects they might have, even though we know these vaccines are safe and effective. So nowadays, one of my jobs is tracking not just the spread of disease, but the spread of false information about disease. I want to understand why lies spread faster and farther than the truth and why people will believe a lie over the truth.

The other thing that I do is I teach doctors and nurses and medical students how to effectively communicate with the people they are caring for. That includes things like how to speak with compassion and empathy with their patients, but also with the public and journalists, so that we can try and get control of the false information that is being spread. I believe that if we have doctors and nurses who are amazing communicators and connectors, we can protect people from becoming "infected" with lies about vaccines.

I'm also a professor at UCLA, where I teach crisis management and crisis communication. And I also write books of nonfiction and poetry. So those are some of the things I do!

What skills are the most important for you to know to do all these jobs?

Two of the most important skills are creativity and open mindedness. These are really important regardless of what you do in life. Creativity is really important for problem solving whether that's as a disease detective, a journalist, or a doctor. I think being creative and open minded makes you a lot more effective at your job. Another important thing I would add to that is being able to work well with people. Being a great listener and an effective communicator are really important too.

What do you like best about your jobs?

I like the feeling that whether I am writing a piece of journalism, whether I am teaching, whether I'm tracking false information, that I'm contributing something to try and make the world a safer place and to make people more knowledgeable and more informed so that they can feel safer. I also really enjoy interacting with different kinds of people, whether that's my MBA or medical students, White House staffers, or the people I interview for my reporting.

One of my favorite things about journalism is that you get to be a bit nosey and curious about people's lives. You can ask lots of questions and get people to trust you and open up to you. I find people's lives and beliefs very interesting. Even as I track the spread of false information, when people believe really absurd, bizarre things about vaccines, it's actually really interesting to me to get to know them and to understand, where does this belief come from? I've made a career out of it!

What did you study in college?

I did my undergraduate degree in biochemistry at Queen Mary University of London. And then I did medical school at Cambridge University. I came to the United States in 2010 to work in the Epidemic Intelligence Service. After that, I studied journalism at the University of Toronto. I'll forever be a student of something!

What do you know now that you wish you had known at age ten?

That everything is achievable! Because what happened to me, Julia, and I hope this never happens to you, is when I was in my teens and I was becoming more interested in epidemics, especially the HIV pandemic, I started to think, oh, I could go to school to become a doctor. But when I was in high school, I had a teacher tell me that I should not bother applying to medical school because I would never get in. And I believed her because no one in my family is a doctor and my family is not very academic.

I come from a single parent family. My mum worked many jobs and studied very hard to get a degree and take care of me at the same time. People in my family don't really go to University, let alone to medical school. My teacher's thinking was, oh, you can only be a successful doctor if you come from a family of doctors or at least if your family is academic and they send people to University. But my family back in England is working class, and not everyone goes to University. But that didn't mean that I couldn't be a doctor.

By telling me, "Don't go to medical school," the teacher impacted my thinking and my ambitions. Instead of applying to medical school, I thought I would try and make a difference in the world in a different way. I thought to myself, "I'll study science and I'll be a scientist. But I won't be a doctor."

But then an amazing person who was a famous doctor met me, recognized my drive and enthusiasm, and told me that I could be a doctor. His name was Dr. Joep Lange. He was a doctor who cared for people living with HIV and AIDS. Because of his conviction and my mum's support, not only did I apply to medical school, but I applied to the two best and most competitive medical schools in the world: Oxford and Cambridge!

I ended up going to Cambridge University to study medicine but it was delayed. I could have gone sooner had my teacher not discouraged me.

But had I known when I was ten that if you really put your mind to something, you can achieve it, even when others doubt you, then I would have known: let the haters be your fuel! When they doubt you, double down in your conviction that you can be anything and do anything that you put your mind to!

Now I know this and I live my life doing everything that I love and enjoy. I don't care if people doubt me. I still get rejected from some things for really absurd reasons. I'll give you one example. My first book came out in 2018. It's about Dr. Lange, the really amazing scientist who was my inspiration and mentor.

Sadly, he passed away in a plane that was shot down by Russian separatists in 2014. So I wrote a book about his life and the amazing discoveries he made which led to medicines that saved the lives of millions of people with HIV. And I was so happy when this book got published and delighted when an audiobook publisher said, "We're buying the rights. We're going to turn your book into an audiobook." I love audiobooks. I said, "I'm happy to narrate it." And they said, "Well, it's a book about science, so we don't want a woman to narrate it. We want a man."

The very next year, something similar happened. A television production company was taking the pilot around to different TV networks, and the bosses at one of them said, "This pilot is great. We don't have enough TV shows on this topic. But the host of this show cannot be a woman because it's about science. We need a host who is a man." That incensed me. But it also gave me a lot of fuel, because in ten or twenty years' time, I do not want you to hear the same kinds of misogynistic* rejections that I am hearing today.

Is there a quote or an inspirational thought or anything like that that motivates you?

Dream so big that your dreams seem absurd! Keep going, keep building, keep dreaming. Never stop. Sometimes you won't realize that you can do something until you see someone else do it. Like you writing a book! Imagine all of the other ten-year-old girls who are going to see that you did this and then feel like, "Wait, I can do it too!"

> **"Keep going, keep building, keep dreaming. Never stop."**
>
> —Dr. Seema Yasmin

---

* Misogynistic means being prejudiced against, or talking down to, women.

Military

now

THEN

Vernice "Flygirl" Armour

America's First Black Female Combat Pilot, First Black Female Pilot in the U.S. Marine Corps, Entrepreneur, Investor, Police Officer, Keynote Speaker

📍 **Georgia**

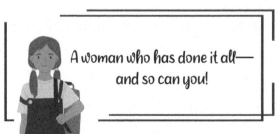

A woman who has done it all—and so can you!

Hello, Flygirl! You were the first African American naval aviator in the Marines and the first female in the Marines to fly in combat. And now a professional speaker. So, tell us briefly about both of those jobs.

Being a pilot of an attack helicopter was like a rollercoaster without wheels. You could go up, down, side to side. It was amazing. It took me a year and a half to get through flight school and just a little while after flight, well, less than sixty days, is when 9/11 happened, and shortly thereafter I found myself flying in the middle of combat. So, things happened very quickly.

With being a professional speaker, sometimes it's like a rollercoaster as well. When you think of where we are right now, just coming through COVID, the whole world has shifted, industries have shifted. With speaking, who knew that what I do relied on large groups of people getting together? So, even the world of speaking has transformed and evolved over the years, decades. It was different in the '70s, '80s, and '90s, and now we're in the 2000s. So, it's just like anything else. How do you stay relevant no matter where you are and what you're doing?

What skills were the most important for you to do your jobs?

I would say some of the skills that would relate to both are focus, courage, resilience, and great communication. As a helicopter pilot there were skills like knowing how to take off and how to land! How to navigate when somebody's shooting at me, how to communicate with the troops on the ground, how to work all the systems inside of the aircraft.

As a professional speaker, how to communicate effectively, how to do storytelling, how to talk to people before I go speak to understand their business and what they do. So, when I talk to their audience, I'm able to relate their story to my story. Or you know how sometimes you do the activity where you connect the dots, where you go from one to two to three and you draw the lines? Same exact thing. You have to connect the dots for people with ideas.

What do you like best about your job? Or what did you like best?

What I loved best about being a combat pilot and being a police officer and being a speaker was that every day is different and I get to meet amazing people along the way, kind of like you.

What did you study in college, and where did you go?

When I first started college, I majored in animal science, with an emphasis on horse science. Because I wanted to be a horse trainer, and ever since I was four years old, I wanted to be a police officer that rode a horse downtown. At the age of six, I got my very first pony and went, "Yes! I am halfway there." After, I think, my first semester, I wasn't on the equestrian team anymore, and I ended up getting involved in the army and I knew I wanted to be a police officer. So I started looking at the military and then I withdrew from school to go into the military for a little bit. Then I went back to school. So I switched my major to physical education with an emphasis in exercise science because I didn't want to major in history or English or biology because I really wanted to major in something that I was passionate about in life and that I felt would also serve me in life. Since I wanted to be a police officer, I felt physical fitness and being in shape and being strong would serve me in life, not just as a police officer, but to keep my body healthy. So, I switched to exercise science and I graduated from Middle Tennessee State University.

What do you know now that you wish you had known at age ten?

When I was ten, I think I was actually getting bullied in school a little bit. What I wish I knew then that I know now is more how to stand up for myself and speak up for myself and still be okay.

What is the one best piece of advice you have for young girls who will be going to high school or college soon?

Always listen to that inner voice, the voice in your head that knows the right thing to do. Sometimes, it might feel scary to do the right thing, but as Dr. Martin Luther King Jr. would say, "It's always the right time to do the right thing." And I call it your gut, that inner voice. And it's the gutsy move. In your gut, you know it's right. It takes guts to do it, but you've got to take action.

That Martin Luther King Jr. quote is wonderful. Can you tell me about a professional or personal setback you had, how you overcame it, and what you learned from it?

Yes. When I was in the military and we were deployed, things slowed down while I was in the middle of combat. So, we weren't flying as much. And the lead instructor said, "Okay, we're going to start studying again and we got a tactics test." And I was like, "Whoa, wait a minute. I haven't been studying." He's like, "Well, you should always be studying." So, long story short, I ended up failing that tactics test. When you're in a highly competitive environment like that, when you fail a tactics test, they don't keep you on the fast track. It's almost like when you're in NASCAR and you get in an accident and you kind of go off to the side, everybody else keeps on going and you have to go into the pit for a little bit to get some repairs. So, instead of staying on the fast track, I got put on the normal track and I ended up going to headquarters Marine Corps, which was cool, but I still wanted to be out there, going to combat and flying.

But what happened is, while I was at headquarters Marine Corps, my dad was diagnosed with cancer and I was able to go home and visit him a whole bunch. One time, my mom's birthday was coming up and I just went home on a surprise and she asked me to come home and I wasn't going to go. And I was like, "Well." Dad was in the hospital and his numbers weren't great. So, I decided to fly home and surprise both of them. While I was there, unfortunately, my dad passed away.

But here's the thing. Had I been in that other squadron, I would've been in Iraq or somewhere else. And all that time I spent regretting failing that test and regretting not being in the squadron anymore, I finally got that the detour is the path. We're exactly where we're supposed to be all the time. And it's, where is the opportunity inside of the obstacle? Because life will always be challenging. We will always have challenges in life. The question is, are we willing to create the opportunity out of the obstacles?

"Always listen to that inner voice, the voice in your head that knows the right thing to do."

—Vernice "Flygirl" Armour

Philanthropy

Cynthia Germanotta

(Lady Gaga's Mom)
President, Born This
Way Foundation

📍 New York, New York

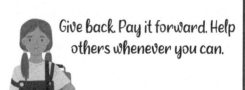

Give back. Pay it forward. Help
others whenever you can.

Hello, Cynthia! You are the president of the Born This Way Foundation. What is the Born This Way Foundation, and what does the president do?

Born This Way Foundation is a nonprofit organization that my daughter Stefani (Lady Gaga) and I co-founded in 2012. Our mission is to inspire and empower young people to build a kinder, braver world. Our foundation was born out of my daughter's mental health journey and her desire to help other young people be better equipped to deal with their struggles than she felt that she was. Our work lies at the intersection of kindness and mental health. Through high-impact programming, youth-led conversations, and strategic, cross-sectoral partnerships, the foundation aims to make kindness cool, validate the emotions of young people, and eliminate the stigma surrounding mental health.

In my role as president of Born This Way Foundation, I perform a wide variety of duties, some of which are required by law and others that are necessary to carry out our mission. Some of my responsibilities are laid out in our bylaws, which require me to perform certain duties to comply with being a tax-exempt organization. In addition, I report to and chair our Board of Directors, preside over board meetings, and oversee finances, vision, mission, staffing, and long-term goal-setting. I also assist with key fundraising and partnerships. It's important that I work closely with our Executive Director and other team members in all of these areas, so we are prepared to make important decisions and execute on our plan.

I'm honored that my daughter asked me to go on this journey with her and I consider myself a steward of her vision for a kinder, braver world; I'm so proud of her for using her platform for good to help other youth.

What skills are the most important for someone in your role to know?

In my role as president and board chair, it's essential to have good leadership and decision-making skills. Even though I did not have direct experience in the nonprofit sector, I had a career for over twenty-five years in the corporate world before my daughter and I co-founded Born This Way Foundation, which gave me the opportunity to develop these and other skills. I have learned a great deal about the nonprofit sector in the last ten years and continue to learn each and every day.

It's important to me to empower others to be great at what they do, while acknowledging their work and value. I do my best to lead by example and listen to the needs of my team, and I would hope that my team would say that I don't lead them but work alongside them. If I need to do the coffee run, I do the coffee run. If I need to speak at the United Nations, I speak at the United Nations. I take the opportunities that I am given in service to our mission and work to create opportunities for others.

What do you like best about your role?

I feel very blessed to have this role and enjoy so many aspects of our work. If I had to choose what I like the best and what brings me the most joy and hope, it would be working with young people all over the world. Young people inspired the foundation and are why we do this great work, and they are very integral to shaping our vision and programs. It was important to my daughter that our work be informed by the unique perspectives and experiences of young people, and as such, our work has been and will always be research-based, youth-focused, and youth-led. I've had the opportunity to speak with and learn from young people everywhere about what is important to them in relation to building kind communities, their mental health and well-being, the tools and resources they need to thrive, and how they envision building the kinder, braver world we know is possible.

What did you study in school, and where did you go?

In school, I studied business and international relations, languages, and public administration. I was fortunate that my parents worked very hard to ensure that their children had the opportunity to go to college. I grew up in West Virginia and completed undergraduate studies at West Virginia University (WVU), including a study abroad program in France. My master's degree is from The George Washington University in Washington, D.C. I have also studied dance for many years and was a member of the WVU dance company, Orchesis.

What do you know now that you wish you had known at age ten?

I have no regrets in life, as I feel that we always have the opportunity to learn from all of our experiences, including our mistakes. Life is a journey to be enjoyed and surprised by, and it's important to be open minded. One thing I wish I knew is that life would definitely present many challenges and that it's important to learn to manage those challenges with as much kindness, grace, and love as possible. Life is also precious and should be lived to the fullest with as much compassion, empathy, and connection as possible. No matter how dark and cold things may feel, remember that there is always light and warmth ahead. Be patient, have hope, and keep moving forward. You will make it through whatever challenges you are facing with the right support. Always have someone to turn to. The sun will come out again.

What is one best piece of advice you have for young girls who will be going to high school, college, and joining the workforce in the next decade or so?

The best piece of advice I can give young girls who will be going to high school, college, and joining the workforce in the next decade or so is to believe in yourself and your capabilities. You bring much value to this world and equally deserve opportunities for your voice to be heard and your talents to be seen and utilized. If you hear no, question it, ask why, pivot, learn, and try again and again.

Remember that you never have to face your struggles alone and that it's important and so helpful to find someone who will be there for you—whether that's a mentor, a trusted advisor, a friend, or sibling, find someone you can rely on who will be there for you.

Is there a quote, an inspirational thought, or anything like that that motivates you each day?

Life is a gift and we are only given one opportunity to live it and contribute. One of the inspirational quotes and thoughts that motivates me is the following:

"Today is a day that will never come again. Make it a great one."

Is there anything you would like to add that we are not asking here?

Let's treat one another with kindness and respect. The world will be a better place if we accept one another's uniqueness and are tolerant and accepting of our differences. Take a minute to do something kind for someone else, especially for someone who would least expect it. Extend a hand and build a bridge to someone who you may think is very different from you. You may be surprised that they are not—we are all just people finding our way.

We can all make the world a little better by the actions we take each day. We can choose to love, to be kind, and to help others. We can make a difference in this world, no matter how small it may seem. Every act of kindness counts and every act of love makes the world a little brighter.

> **"Remember that you never have to face your struggles alone..."**
>
> —Cynthia Germanotta

Risk Management

now

THEN

Meredith Wilson

Chief Executive Officer, Emergent Risk International

📍 **Newport, Rhode Island**

The power of thinking differently!

Hello! You are the chief executive officer for Emergent Risk International. What is that, and what do you do?

I used to work for the U.S. government as an intelligence analyst. I did a lot of research and wrote a lot of papers related to security issues—politics, risk, that kind of thing. And now my company does similar work, but mostly for other companies. So, let's say you've got a company that has an office in a place like Afghanistan, or Poland, or the Philippines, and so forth. And they want to know what the security situation is like. Are there places to be avoided? Is there anything that could impact the safety of their employees or business operations? That sort of thing. We help them understand that and then we help them think about ways to keep people safe. In the beginning, when I started the company, I did everything. I wrote papers, called up companies and told them what we did. But now we have many more employees and people working with us all over the world.

What skills are most important for you to know to do your job?

It's really important to have good writing skills. You have to be able to communicate in writing, but it's just as important to have good verbal skills and the ability to work with people. To really be able to understand what people need and to be able to listen to what's important to them. Business skills are also important, but I've learned those as I go. I think that about 80 percent of my job is about communication, whether it's writing or talking to people or working with people.

What do you like best about your job?

I think what I like the most is that I get to create jobs for people and that I get to do something new almost every day.

There's rarely a day that goes by that I don't learn something new. It's the variety of things that I get to do that also make me happy and keep me motivated.

What did you study in college, and where did you go?

I started off at Michigan State and then I left school for three or four years. I traveled around the world, and that was my real college—the college of traveling abroad. And when I came back, I went to the University of Arizona, and that was when I discovered what I really wanted to do, which was some sort of international relations–type work. So I later went to work for the government. I went to Malaysia and did my master's degree there.

What do you know now that you wish you had known at age ten?

Well, a couple of things come to mind. The first is that I wish I knew then how powerful I could be. And I wish I understood then that the little things that were hard day to day would be really important to me becoming who I am. I think probably the other thing is that I wish I knew to just relax and have fun! I was one of those kids that wanted to be an adult when I was like, five. And so I always wanted to hang out with the adults and talk to the adults. You do learn a lot when you're precocious like that!

What is one best piece of advice that you have for girls who will be going to college and eventually joining the workforce?

I think there's a couple of really important things. One is to be creative and think a little bit differently than what everybody else is talking about. Think about what the future looks like.

And, and also remember that you can do your own thing and to know that the sky's the limit. That's one of the really great things about America, that you can do that. Think about not just getting a job one day—but think about what you could do, what you could create. What kind of things, what kind of value do you have to give the world?

I focus on this a lot with my kids, because after my last job [at an energy company], I decided that job security was really kind of an illusion. And I wanted them to understand that jobs will be different in twenty years. In twenty years there will probably be more entrepreneurism, so I think helping kids understand what it means to run a business and what it means to be self-sufficient is really important.

If you go back to 1990, for example, nobody had ever heard of Google or Amazon. These are world-changing companies. They've disrupted everything, and they didn't even exist when I was thinking about my future career. And I think that kind of thing is only going to accelerate. And that's one thing I think that girls really need to know is that the world that we see today is not the world that's going to exist in ten or fifteen years! It's all going to be very different, so you have to be creative and nimble.

Kids today hear a lot about climate change, and there are going to be some very real—and very hard—lessons there. But they should also understand that some really cool things are going to happen in the next twenty or thirty years. Pay attention to those things because that might be where your opportunity lies. It's also important to remember that in times of crisis and disruption, people innovate—and that's how opportunities can be created.

Is there a quote or an inspirational thought or anything like that that motivates you each day?

"Travel is fatal to prejudice, bigotry, and narrow-mindedness, and many of our people need it sorely on these accounts. Broad, wholesome, charitable views of men and things cannot be acquired by vegetating in one little corner of the earth all one's lifetime." —Mark Twain

Can you tell me about a professional or personal setback you had, how you overcame it, and what you learned from it?

Oh yes, girl! My career (and most people's careers) is littered with professional setbacks, but in a good way. I think that almost every really important professional experience that I've had or really learned from has been learned from the school of hard knocks. The one that led me to launch my company was actually a layoff where my company decided to downsize and they decided to eliminate my job. It was really hard because they had recruited me for the position and moved my whole family, and about a year in, they said, see ya. But I had a boss at the time that sat me down and said, you know, I really think you ought to start your own company. You've got the brains for it. It turned out to be the best thing I've ever done professionally.

> **"The world that we see today is not the world that's going to exist in ten or fifteen years!"**
>
> —Meredith Wilson

Sports

Cynthia Marshall

Chief Executive Officer, Dallas Mavericks, National Basketball Association

📍 **Dallas, Texas**

Rising to the top in professional sports.

Hello! You are the chief executive officer of the Dallas Mavericks! Wow! What do you do? Please tell me about your job.

My job is to run the business side of basketball. I am neither scout nor coach. I lead the team that is responsible for profitability of the Dallas Mavericks, one of the NBA's thirty professional basketball teams. I make sure that we make money and do it in a way that is honest and ethical and takes care of our employees, fans, and other stakeholders.

My team ensures a full arena of twenty thousand fans for forty-one home games and presents a spectacular game experience.

We are responsible for marketing and branding the team, including our social media presence, and securing sponsors.

I am also responsible for the player relations, human resources, legal, information technology, financial, and analytics aspects of our business.

I lead approximately two hundred people.

What skills are the most important for you to know to do your job?

Several things are important:

- Ability to provide a vision and strategic direction
- Ability to communicate effectively
- Ability to assemble a strong team
- Be a role model and instill a set of uncompromising values that guide our daily actions
- Have agility and the ability to pivot quickly, especially during difficult and unexpected situations (e.g., global pandemic)

- Have great interpersonal skills and ability to genuinely love people and show empathy and compassion
- Have the ability to analyze data and make good and timely decisions relative to our people, financials, etc.

What do you like best about your job?

I LOVE interacting with people. I love helping my employees grow in their careers and in their personal lives. I love talking to our players and spending time with our fans at games.

I am very competitive and therefore I like setting goals to be the best in our industry and then executing on the plans related to the goals.

I like having a voice in the sports world to help women and girls and to help improve the success of women in sports.

I like having a platform that naturally unifies people. We can use it for good things, and we do.

What did you study in college, and where did you go?

I attended the University of California at Berkeley and studied business administration and human resources management.

What do you know now that you wish you had known at age ten?

I wish I knew that the world was bigger than just my neighborhood, and one day I would have an opportunity to contribute to something much larger than my Richmond, CA universe.

What is the one best piece of advice you have for young girls who will be going to high school, college, and joining the workforce in the next decade or so?

Be open to the possibilities of how you will impact the world. Don't get locked in too early on what you think you will be doing for the rest of your life. Your talents, gifts, education, and experiences will be used in ways that you probably can't imagine right now. So just develop your foundation (talents, gifts, education, and experiences), and look forward to how things will unfold. There is a plan for your life that will be revealed over time.

Can you tell me about a professional or personal setback you had, how you overcame it, and what you learned from it?

Once I was promoted into a very big operational role when I worked at AT&T. I decided it was important for me to spend time with and thus get to know ALL of the people in my organization. This required lots of field visits because I was responsible for several hundreds of people at different levels, from technicians who climbed the telephone poles to their supervisors and managers. I really wanted to understand their work so I could know how to serve them and know how to serve our customers.

I had a motto that said, "People work by day and paper work by night," meaning I would handle all of my administrative work at the end of the day or when I got home. The people came first.

Well, I went overboard with that philosophy and failed to pay attention to some important reports until it was too late. One night, I really dialed in on the data in a report and found some discrepancies. Instead of making field visits the next day, I stayed in the office and asked lots of questions about the reports. I went back in time in my research and found a disturbing trend. As a result, I had to take disciplinary action on an employee who was engaged in unethical behavior.

The lesson is that had I done a better job balancing ALL aspects of my job, I think I would have discovered the problem sooner. So now, whenever I start a new position, I try to get a firm grasp on the scope of my job, ways to measure success, reports involved, who are the people, etc. And then I integrate the people-work and the paperwork (aka administrative tasks). I very much appreciate the full job and the need to structure my time to do all of it well, every day.

Is there a quote, an inspirational thought, or anything like that that motivates you each day?

"People don't care how much you know until they know how much you care" is my favorite quote. It has been attributed to President Theodore Roosevelt.

Is there anything you would like to add that we are not asking here?

I have four words that I live by: dream, focus, pray, and act.

My leadership philosophy is that in order to be a successful leader, I need to do three things: *listen* to the people, *learn* from the people, and *love* the people. That's Cynt's Three Ls of Leadership.

I attribute my success to my mother, who put two books in my hands at an early age: a math book and a bible.

I believe we are a team and we are supposed to help each other. No man/woman is an island. We need each other.

Teamwork matters. And the team looks like everyone (all races, ethnicities, genders, socioeconomic status, abilities, etc.).

> "I have four words that I live by: dream, focus, pray, and act."
>
> —Cynthia Marshall

Benita Fitzgerald Mosley

 Olympic Gold Medalist; Vice President, Community & Impact, and President, FundPlay, LeagueApps

📍 Virginia

 Winning on the field —and off it!

Hello! You are an Olympic gold medal champion from the 1984 Los Angeles Olympics, and also a sports executive. That's so exciting! Please tell me what you are doing now.

I'm the vice president of Community and Impact for League-Apps. Also president of FundPlay, their philanthropic arm. And LeagueApps is a youth sports management technology platform. So organizers of youth clubs and leagues and tournaments use LeagueApps to run their organizations.

What skills are most important for you to know to do your job?

I would say first and foremost, leadership skills. You have to be skilled and experienced in running organizations. Running, in my case, nonprofit organizations. Also, a background in engineering is helpful. I have an engineering degree (industrial engineering), so as a technology platform, they're a for-profit company. But I'm dealing a lot with, on the philanthropic side, the nonprofit organizations that we're donating our technology to. They help them serve more kids and run their organizations more effectively. So having a background in leadership, background in technology, background in sports, and particularly youth sports, and what issues and challenges youth sports organizers face.

What do you like best about your job?

What I like best about my job is the opportunity to have an impact on communities all across the country. We have almost 120 youth sports organizations that we are benefiting, and they collectively are impacting three-hundred-thousand young people around the country. So these are sports-based nonprofits who are providing free or reduced-cost access to youth sports, to kids who otherwise couldn't afford it in underserved communities.

What did you study in school, and where did you go?

I went to the University of Tennessee on a full athletic scholarship. I ran track. I was a fourteen-time All American. I made two Olympic teams while I was in school. My major, I ended up with a bachelor of science in industrial engineering.

What do you know now that you wish you had known at age ten?

At age ten I had really low self-confidence. I hadn't found my talent and abilities yet. My parents were both educators and they believed in allowing us to experience a lot of trial and error. So I tried all different sports. I tried softball and gymnastics and majorettes. I tried violin and some other instruments I didn't either like or wasn't good at. But by the time I got to middle school, I was able to find out that I was a really good flute player, that I was a really good runner. And so, by age twelve or so, I began to discover what I was good at. So I found out if you just keep trying you'll find it. If you don't succeed, try it again. Just keep trying!

So that's what I wish I knew when I was ten years old. That you just keep trying things and you might fail. You might fall on your face, you might trip over a hurdle, but you get back up and it's the trying that helps you find that success!

What is the one best piece of advice you have for young girls who would be going to high school and college and joining the workforce soon?

So I have this question that I started asking myself back in '84 before the Olympics, and it's "Why not me?" And so I was on the track for training, it was after practice one day. I had made my second Olympic team. I was going to Los Angeles for the Olympics, and I was thinking about kind of visualizing myself in the stadium and I realized that I was thinking about somebody else winning. I was hoping that I was going to make the final or run my personal best time or maybe beat a certain individual, but thinking about myself being in first place and getting the gold medal wasn't occurring to me. And I thought to myself, "Why not me? Why can't I be the one that wins the gold medal? Why not me as the one who's on top of the victory stand, why not me cross the finish line first?"

I felt like I worked hard and I was as talented as any of the other girls that were going to be competing. And so now I just ask myself that question every time those doubts start to creep in. Why not me?

Oftentimes you're going to find yourself in a position where someone either offers you a job or opens up an opportunity to you, and you're going to have to ask yourself, "Why not me?" And encourage yourself to step out of your comfort zone and do some things that you might not feel totally ready for, but once you do it, you're going to be good. And that's the only way to be great, is to get started. You don't have to be great to get started, but you do have to get started to be great.

Can you tell me about a professional or personal setback you've had, how you overcame it, and what you learned from it?

At the beginning of the COVID pandemic, I lost my job. I was CEO of Laureus Sport for Good Foundation USA. I'd been CEO for four years and my job got eliminated because they didn't have the funding to continue paying me and my number two person. For six months I was without a job and I had, thankfully, a backup plan. I had already started consulting with Airbnb, and I started consulting with Proteus. And in those six months, I probably had more job opportunities come my way than I had six years prior to that.

By the summer of the pandemic, when everybody was losing their jobs, I was getting more job opportunities. I ended up with three job offers at the same time. So I guess the biggest setback was having my position eliminated in the middle of a global pandemic and feeling like the world's coming to an end—before realizing it was one of the best things that could have happened to me. I went from running nonprofit organizations to running the philanthropic arm of a for-profit company. So now I have equity in the company. It's a startup, and so it could even financially be a much better reward for me down the line in a few years.

> "You don't have to be great to get started, but you do have to get started to be great."
>
> —Benita Fitzgerald Mosley

Technology and Software

now

THEN

Jeanette Cajide

Vice President of Strategy, Dialexa (an IBM company)

📍 **Dallas, Texas**

> You know what's fun? Working with smart people and making an impact.

Hello! You are the vice president of Strategy at Dialexa. What is Dialexa, and what do you do?

Dialexa is an innovative technology product development firm that helps ambitious companies design and build digital software products and transform the way they do business. As vice president of strategy, I spend my time researching and thinking about ways to grow Dialexa through new services, offerings, and markets. I get to think about the future of the company, determine the existing gaps, and work with the leadership team to help the company build the capabilities that make the future a reality.

What skills and knowledge do you need to have to do your job?

I am what they consider a generalist because my skills and knowledge are diverse. I've accumulated a lot of different business skills over the years, but my job in investment banking is foundational to everything I do. That job taught me financial analysis, market research, and competitive analysis. I also learned to evaluate multiple industries. As a result, I am rarely intimidated by a problem at work, as I know I can figure it out or can find someone who can help me figure it out.

What do you like best about your job?

What I love most about my job are the people. I work with extremely smart people who are obsessed with making an impact in the world. They are also funny and like to have fun. Going to work is fun.

What did you study in college, and where did you go?

I have three college degrees. I have a bachelor of journalism in public relations from the University of Texas at Austin, a master of business administration at Northwestern University Kellogg School of Management, and a master of public administration at Harvard University Kennedy School of Government.

What do you know now that you wish you had known at age ten?

When I was ten, I really cared about what other people thought about me. I moved from Miami to Dallas and I was getting ready to start middle school. I felt so out of place and sad at times because I left all of my friends in Miami. It is natural to want to have friends and be popular, but I think it is more important to have friends who are kind. Pay attention to how your friends treat other people—other kids, teachers, and the staff. This will help you pick the right friends.

What is the one best piece of advice you have for girls who will be going to high school, college, and joining the workforce in the next decade or so?

Do not worry about your major in college, just try to get the best education you possibly can and it will sort itself out. Remember, math is not hard. If you feel that it is, you need a better teacher or tutor to help you figure it out. Once you get it, it will unlock so many paths (engineering, medicine, finance). Find a love for reading. The more you read, the more you can teach yourself about life, history, and experiences. Money is important, but you will spend most of your life working. Learn to look for flow states. A flow state is when you are fully immersed when performing a task. This should be your compass.

Tell me about a personal or professional failure or setback you encountered. How did you overcome it, and what did you learn from it?

I launched my first startup in 2012. Blurtt was the first meme creation app in the Apple app store. Although memes are now ubiquitous, back in 2012, it was still a new way of communicating. I was too early and I had to shut down the company in 2014. Failure is a better teacher than success. This experience helped build my confidence for the next thing because I knew what to watch out for and what better questions to ask.

Is there a quote, an inspirational thought, or anything like that that motivates you each day?

"The vision that you glorify in your mind, the ideal that you enthrone in your heart—this you will build your life by, and this you will become." —James Lane Allen

> "It is natural to want to have friends and be popular, but I think it is more important to have friends who are kind. Pay attention to how your friends treat other people—other kids, teachers, and the staff. This will help you pick the right friends."
>
> —Jeannette Cajide

Jakita Owensby Thomas

 Phillpott Westpoint Stevens
Distinguished Professor
of Computer Science and
Software Engineering,
Auburn University

📍 **Auburn, Alabama**

The world runs on
software.

Hello! You are a professor of computer science and software engineering at Auburn University. Wow! Tell me about your job.

I am the Phillpott Westpoint Stevens Distinguished Professor of Computer Science and Software Engineering at Auburn University. My job involves designing and teaching courses in computer science and software engineering, conducting research, engaging in service to the Auburn community as well as the computer science community, and mentoring students.

What skills are the most important for you to know to do your job?

Being a professor is like running your own company. You have to be really good at managing your time, managing multiple tasks, and you must have really good critical thinking and problem-solving skills, because every day is different and produces new challenges and opportunities.

What do you like best about your job?

What I love best about my job is that I get to play a role in the development of the next generation of computer scientists and software engineers. I also love that I get to investigate areas that I'm passionate about through my research and service.

What did you study in college, and where did you go?

I attended Spelman College in Atlanta, GA, for my undergraduate studies, and I received a bachelor of science in computer information sciences with a minor in mathematics. I received my PhD in computer science from the Georgia Institute of Technology (Georgia Tech).

What do you know now that you wish you had known at age ten?

At age ten, I thought I wanted to be a pediatrician, so I would tell my ten-year-old self to always keep an open mind because you might find something you love a lot more that suits you better.

What is the one best piece of advice you have for young girls who will be going to high school, college, and joining the workforce in the next decade or so?

Always let your passion lead. A lot of people will try to tell you what they think is best for you and your future. Always trust your gut and that voice inside you. You have everything inside you that it takes to make your dreams come true. Just follow your passion, and you'll find success!

Is there a quote, an inspirational thought, or anything like that that motivates you each day?

"Do all you can, when you can, while you can."

Tell me about a professional or personal setback. How did you overcome it, and what did you learn from that?

When I was in my early twenties, I competed for Miss Fulton County, and I won first runner up. It was the last year I was eligible to compete, and I was very disappointed. However, I'd made some wonderful friends that I still have to this day, and I also received lots of scholarship money as well. I learned that things may not always go as you plan, but there's always something to be learned from every situation. Sometimes, you gain things that end up being more valuable.

"There's always something to be learned from every situation."

—Jakita Owensby Thomas

now

THEN

Tonya Walley

Vice President of Field Operations Strategy, Cox Communications

📍 **Herndon, Virginia**

Going from climbing utility poles to climbing the corporate ladder.

Hello! You are the vice president of Field Operations for Cox Communications. What is that, and what do you do?

Field Operations is all about connecting our customers to the things that matter most. In Field Operations, we are responsible for installing and maintaining products and services that connect customers. For example, we install routers for internet and phone connectivity, cable boxes to connect to broadcast channels, and products that also help customers secure their properties. Our customers are both residential and commercial. We are also responsible for plant maintenance, which is critical, as this infrastructure is what enables our products and services to work.

The vice president of operations sets the strategy, vision, and goals for the team and empowers the team to meet those goals. The vice president is also responsible for advocating for the team and removing roadblocks that inhibit progress of the team. I often refer to this role as coach as a lot of what we are responsible for is calling plays and modifying strategies to reach our organizational goals.

What skills are the most important for someone in your role to know?

The skills most important for someone in my role are: impeccable people leadership skills; business acumen; an understanding of telephony and/or cable infrastructure; understanding of the customer landscape; and the ability to build relationships, collaborate, and influence others to get things done.

What do you like best about your role?

There are so many things I love about my role, but I will give you my top three. First, I love the people-leadership aspect.

As an altruistic person, I absolutely love people, and love inspiring them to be their best. I particularly love developing, mentoring, and advising my team and my extended team. I also love taking care of our customers, which speaks to my love of helping to make the lives of others better. So in this role I am able to fuel my passion and live in my purpose of enhancing the lives of others. The last thing I will share is that in this role I am able to connect to a bigger purpose and help move our business forward, which excites me on a daily basis.

What did you study in school?

Well, I am sort of a career student and a consummate learner, so my education is pretty exhaustive, but not all required for this role. For my undergrad, I studied at St. Peter's College in Jersey City, NJ; my major was computer science and I graduated Cum Laude. From there I attended an engineering school, Stevens Institute of Technology in Hoboken, NJ, and earned double master's degrees, first in telecommunications management, with a concentration in wireless management, and the other in network engineering. Next up, I attended Cornell and received a financial management certificate in 2016. This year, I completed a certificate at Harvard Business School in strategy and execution. In addition to my formal education, I have attended numerous leadership classes, which have helped me strengthen my business and leadership acumen.

What do you know now that you wish you had known at age ten?

Thinking back to when I was ten, and compared to now, I have always been an introvert and somewhat a shy girl. I now know how important it is to flex between introversion and extroversion. Relationships are at the core of everything we do, whether professional or personal, they are super important and must be nourished and maintained with intentionality. So at the age of ten, although many of us were not thinking about relationship building, I wish I would have known how important that would eventually be to my growth.

What is the one best piece of advice you have for young girls who will be going to high school, college, and joining the workforce in the next decade or so?

One piece of advice I would offer up is to dream so big that it scares the life out of you. When I say scare the life out of you, we all have a dream of what we want our lives to be and often we are afraid to follow those dreams, perhaps because they intimidate us. So I want you to dream so big that it does scare that life right out of you and that dream comes to fruition. As you are dreaming, be purposeful about creating relationships that will help you reach those dreams and make sure you are giving back in a meaningful way…. I am a firm believer, what you put into the universe will return to you. Sow great seeds, reap great harvest!

Is there a quote, an inspirational thought, or anything like that that motivates you each day?

Absolutely! I love quotes and inspirational thoughts but for me what is most motivating are my daily affirmations. Oftentimes, women find themselves in a place of doubt about their abilities, or unsure of themselves, so it is so important that you have a healthy narrative about yourself that will filter out the noises of doubt. So I have a list of ten affirmations stored in my phone that I can refer to every single day, and they motivate, uplift, and remind me of who I am and where I am headed.

Can you tell me about a professional or personal setback you had, how you overcame it, and what you learned from it?

The date was December 12, 1989. I was in my first year of college, preparing for my first semester of final exams, how daunting. Well, equally challenging was that I was studying for those exams in an ICU waiting room as my mother lay dying only a few hundred feet away. First year of college classes consisted of calculus, physics, chemistry, etc., need I say more?! And then, the announcement that my mother had passed away. My soul was crushed!

I did take my exams and managed to finish that semester with a B, although barely. Next semester I dropped out of college and started the journey of healing. So what was an immediate setback to my educational goals eventually became one of the biggest lessons about myself. Through this process, I learned the words resiliency and perseverance and have carried those superpowers with me throughout my life and career.

Is there anything you would like to add that we are not asking here?

It is so important you identify what you are passionate about. Listen to your heart and determine what makes it sing. I share that my passions are people, in particular leading, developing, and mentoring them to bring the best out of them. Because I have identified my passions and purpose, it makes the roles I choose so much easier to navigate and be successful in.

I believe when you are following your passions and purpose, the work is not work, it is your higher calling. I believe we are all here and have a predestined purpose for our lives. If you are not sure about your purpose or passion, start with doing something good in your community. For me, fighting food insecurity is part of my purpose in life, and it allows me to give back to my community in such meaningful ways as well as enhance the lives of others.

> "If you are not sure about your purpose or passion, start with doing something good in your community."
>
> —Tonya Walley

Transportation

now

THEN

Diana Marina Cooper

Global Head of Policy & Regulations, Supernal (a division of Hyundai Air Mobility)

📍 Washington, D.C.

"Flying cars" are going to be huge: a $1 trillion industry by 2040.[10]

Hello, Diana! What is Supernal, and tell me about flying cars!

Hyundai Air Mobility is developing electric "flying cars" that have the potential to radically transform the way people live, work, and play. This emerging technology, referred to as "Advanced Air Mobility," will help humanity live more equitable and sustainable lives for future generations to come.

My role at Hyundai is focused on working with lawmakers, policymakers, regulators, industry, and communities to develop the legal and policy framework to support the introduction of Advanced Air Mobility and to drive public acceptance of this emerging technology.

What skills are most important for you to know to do your job?

The skills that are most important for my career in Government Affairs are communication, negotiation, coalition building, creativity, and persuasion. Additionally, I rely on developing in-depth knowledge of issues that impact the aviation and transportation industries such as safety, security, privacy, and federalism.

What do you like best about your job?

There are very few technological innovations that will stand the test of time and make the history books, some examples of these innovations include cars, planes, the internet, and the cell phone. I believe that Advanced Air Mobility is one of these transformational technologies that will fundamentally shape society for generations to come, and it's a privilege to dedicate my career to help usher in this new revolution in mobility.

What did you study in college, and where did you go?

I studied politics and governance at Ryerson University (Toronto, Ontario, Canada). After completing my bachelor's degree, I went on to pursue a master's in globalization studies at McMaster University (Hamilton, Ontario, Canada), where I focused my research on the impacts of Chinese trade and investment in Sub-Saharan Africa. Afterwards, I completed a JD in law and technology at the University of Ottawa.

What do you know now that you wish you had known at age ten?

From a young age, I felt pressure from teachers, parents, and schoolmates to take courses that would look good on paper that would position me for college, or law school or passing the bar. In high school, I was advised to pursue advanced math and science, even though I didn't like those subjects and I wasn't very good at them. Rather than taking additional courses in English, history, and civics, which I enjoyed and excelled at, I struggled to fit the mold, and my grades and outlook suffered. In law school, I faced similar pressures to take core courses to help me prepare for taking the bar or landing at the right law firm, but this time I chose a different path.

While many of my classmates were taking courses on evidence and civil procedure, I was receiving credits for writing about robots. Following my passion served me well—it made my educational experience much more enjoyable and it also sparked my career in drones and Advanced Air Mobility.

What is the one best piece of advice you have for girls who will be going to high school, college, and joining the workforce in the next decades?

Education is about the journey and the journey can feel very long if it doesn't inspire you. The same is true for your profession. My advice for you as you start thinking about your career is to be bold, pursue meaningful work, and work hard. Define your own path in a field that truly excites you. If that path is uncharted and no one else is leading it—even better, because emerging fields offer unique opportunities for younger generations like yours. In these emerging fields, there are no leading experts with decades of experience for you to compete with. We are in an era of rapid innovation in technology and business models—think of Advanced Air Mobility, hyperloops,* and cryptocurrencies.† These innovations are transforming the world around us and the ways in which the workforce is engaged, creating the jobs of the future—the jobs of your future.

Is there an inspirational quote that motivates you?

"The most courageous act is still to think for yourself. Aloud." —*Coco Chanel*

---

* The term used to describe high-speed transportation systems.

† A cryptocurrency is a digital system of money. Payments and records are made and protected with cryptography instead of by a central authority like a government or a bank.

"Emerging fields offer unique opportunities..."

—Diana Marina Cooper

Travel and Tourism

Kristin Kitchen

 Chief Executive Officer, Sojourn Heritage Accommodations

📍 Cincinnati, Ohio

 How cool would it be to own a hotel?

Hello! You are the chief executive officer of Sojourn Heritage Accommodations. What do you do?

In short: everything! We are an emerging brand, so I have to be all things...from front desk, to housekeeping, to meeting with million-dollar investors about the future of our brand and where we plan to open our next hotels. This involves a lot of strategy and planning, studying the markets of primary and secondary tourism markets, speaking to local governments to see what kind of incentive packages they have for development, understanding tax codes, researching permitting laws and community building so that when we do select a city, we know what neighborhoods hold the most history and whose stories we want to share on our walls!

What skills do you think are keys to success?

Determination is key. You have to believe in yourself. I have been self-employed for over twenty-five years and I owe my success to simply never giving up. Being sure about my commitment to being a social entrepreneur and finally finding the partners who believe in my vision enough to assist in making them come true.

Always staying positive is key. I think your outlook on life greatly determines your success or failure.

What did you study in college, and where did you go?

I was a business major in college with a focus in marketing at St. Mary's University in San Antonio, Texas. I studied African American studies post-graduate at the University of Cincinnati.

Julia Taylor Brandus

What do you know now that you wish you had known at age ten?

Julia, this is a very hard question! At ten, life was beautiful! I didn't know about the ills of society that keep us divided, about structural racism and discrimination. I didn't even know how poor we were because I grew up in rural Tennessee where everybody around me was poor. We had what we needed mostly and when we didn't we made do. My parents divorced when I was five, and my mom was an educator at a small Black college in Knoxville, Tennessee. She struggled most of our lives to make ends meet but we had a nice home filled with a lot of love. When the electricity would get cut off she taught us French by candlelight! Instead of being devastated when it happened, my siblings and I would say, "Oooh, we are gonna play French Restaurant tonight!" That was the name we chose. My sister and I would dress up like fancy ladies and my brother would be the maître d' and we would order our imaginary fancy foods off the menus she made for us! We would mess up ALL the words and laugh like crazy! What was really on our plates was probably a peanut butter and jelly sandwich! Can you say peanut butter and jelly in French? It's one of the first things I learned to say! "*Sandwich au beurre de cacahuète et gelée.*"

Now as an adult and a mom of a nine-year-old daughter, I realize how tough it was for her and how amazing it was that she chose to shield us from the weight of poverty and the stress of what was really happening.

Now, back to your question! I wish that I had known that the only acceptance we truly need is self-acceptance. Once you have that, the rest will follow! Do your best and know it is perfectly okay to get a B or a C! Nobody cares when you are fifty if you got straight As in the fourth grade! Your ability to be successful is not determined by those that are grading you but by how you grade yourself.... If you are proud of yourself...let that light shine brightly so others can see it!

What advice would you give to young girls ten years old, or in high school or college?

Don't let anybody tell you that you can't be the CEO!

Tell me about a professional or personal setback and what you learned from it.

When the markets crashed in 2008, my entire financial portfolio was with Lehman Brothers (a bank that wound up going out of business). I remember watching CNN and the reporter said the bank failed. I wasn't even sure what that meant but I knew immediately that it wasn't good. I worried that my whole future was in jeopardy.... I was terrified. I had a pit in my stomach because I had no answers and no one else seemed to have them either. What happens when your bank goes bankrupt?

Then one morning, I woke up and decided to take control of my success or failure! I said out loud the Serenity Prayer. Again...it's mostly how we look at life that determines whether or not we succeed, right? I decided that I needed inspiration. It was January and the slow season for my B&B (I only had one at the time) so I impulsively decided to buy a ticket to Kenya and go and work in an orphanage for two months. I needed to remember what was really important. I worked with children who could get up and praise God every day and they didn't even have parents. I gained strength and understanding from those kids and when it was time to go back I was ready to face the financial crisis knowing that I had everything that was really important and what I was losing was only stuff. I told myself to stop whining and go bail myself out of the crisis. I had to get a job consulting again at a few universities and put myself on the lecture circuit in order to continue to pay the mortgage at my bed and breakfast. I lost my house and several other properties, but I was fine. I was able to keep my dream going and that choice helped me to keep moving forward. But it also taught me a valuable lesson about "stuff" and the importance of balance.

Is there an inspirational quote that motivates you?

I grew up in rural Tennessee with an educator for a mom. We didn't have TV, but we had books. I found a book of poems written by a man named Javan. This poem was one that really stuck with me and I was close to your age when I found it:

> "One day I said to God,
>
> I am going to search the world over to find the meaning of my existence.
>
> I am going to find the talents within me and develop them to the best of my ability.
>
> I am going to make the most of this life that I have been given
>
> And I will do this without infringing on anyone else's opportunities to do the same.
>
> And God replied. 'I couldn't ask for anything else.'"

This poem became my mantra and my measuring stick for self-actualization. "Am I developing my talents to the best of my ability?" is the question that I continue to ask myself, even until this day. But it also helped me to understand that making the most of the life that I have been given is a responsibility and not an option. How we do that has to be in line with our purpose. How we serve others…and how the opportunity to serve is the blessing!

> "I owe my success to simply never giving up."
>
> —Kristin Kitchen

Veterinary and Animal Care

His name is Frank!

Dr. Molly Benner

Veterinarian

📍 **Englewood, Colorado**

Animal lovers wanted!

Hello! You are a veterinarian. Tell me about your job.

Veterinarians are doctors for animals and most commonly take care of family dogs and cats to try to prevent them from getting sick and fix them when they do. It requires another four years of school after college to become a veterinarian, and this is a versatile degree as not all veterinarians decide to be dog and cat doctors.

Veterinarians contribute greatly to our society, in food safety, epidemiology, drug development, cancer research, and even in Congress, just to name a few. Specifically, I am a veterinary oncologist, meaning that I work with dogs and cats that have cancer, and this is a type of specialty medicine.

To become a veterinary specialist, we do at least a one-year internship program after veterinary school followed by a three-year residency.

What skills are the most important for someone in your role to know?

Successful practicing veterinarians need to know a lot. There is both a breadth and depth of knowledge about disease prevention, diagnosis, and treatment in multiple species that is always expanding.

Many veterinarians also have incredible surgical skills—fixing broken bones, twisted intestines, teeth, and tumors. Communication is perhaps the most important skill for veterinarians. Without good communication with pet owners, we may never get to demonstrate our knowledge or show our surgical skills.

What do you like best about your role?

I love animals. I love getting to meet so many new dogs and cats throughout my day, even though it can be quite sad sometimes because many of them are sick. I am a big believer in the human-animal bond, which can inspire such incredible joy, laughter, and connection, and definitely help us through tough times. I love that I get to see and serve it almost every day.

What did you study in college, and where did you go?

I went to the University of North Carolina at Chapel Hill and graduated with a degree in journalism and mass communication. Most veterinarians have college degrees in biology or animal science, and I did have to do some extra schooling before I was accepted to veterinary school for the required science background. I don't regret the extra time and school because I think my journalism degree has served me well in my profession, and I encourage everyone to remember that you can always pivot from your chosen path if it doesn't feel right.

What do you know now that you wish you had known at age ten?

I think this is your toughest question. I am tempted to say that I wish I knew everything then that I know now. But life is a journey as they say, and mistakes are important, so I think it is best that you don't know too much when you're ten. You should know to be kind and open to new experiences and friends. Learn as many languages as you can.

What is the one best piece of advice you have for young girls who will be going to high school, college, and joining the workforce in the next decade or so?

Try your best to avoid substantial student loans.

Is there a quote, an inspirational thought, or anything like that that motivates you each day?

Sometime after college, I had a poster of Muhammad Ali just after he knocked out Sonny Liston in Lewiston, Maine in 1965. It had the words IMPOSSIBLE IS NOTHING. I used to think Ali said that. He didn't. It was supposedly written by an ad copywriter for Adidas around 2004. Doesn't matter, I love it. Honorable mention to Ferris Bueller, from my favorite movie when I was ten, who said, "Life moves pretty fast. If you don't stop and look around once in a while, you could miss it."

Is there anything you would like to add that we are not asking here?

I was ten years old thirty years ago (Ferris Bueller was right, it goes fast!). Being ten in 1991 was vastly different than being ten now. In some ways, I think I had it better and in some ways it's better right now. You have the added wisdom of another generation shaping your formative years, growing in a more inclusive, individualistic, and anti-bully society. Half your class may already be coders and entrepreneurs making a difference and money on the internet. Remember to be a little tough, though. Remember that life is not always up and that a big part of success is how you cope with the down. Remember that nobody owes you anything. Remember that a good sense of humor is free and worth more than most of what you can buy.

"Remember that nobody owes you anything."

—Dr. Molly Benner

Profile Index

Anderson, Leslie, 42
Armour, Vernice, 212
Baker, Jill, 142
Bakhtian, Noël, 96
Ballard, Elizabeth "Beth", 6
Bansal, Rina, 190
Ben-Ghiat, Ruth, 78
Benner, Molly, 276
Berry, Amy, 106
Bollini, Subhashini, 147
Braden, Jean, 195
Cai, Mei, 100
Cajide, Jeanette, 246
Cheng, Marguerita, 54
Cline, Julia, 16
Conroy, Carmela, 116
Cooper, Diana Marina, 262
Doirin, Schelo, 58
Dowd, Maureen, 130
Earman, Susan Friedlander, 153
Fitzgerald Mosley, Benita, 240

Germanotta, Cynthia, 220

Greenspan, Emily, 172

Helt, Gail, 82

Hennessy, Jill, 180

Hunter, Constance, 63

Ibrahim, Sandy, 200

Jones-Oliveira, Janet, 46

Kim, Amy, 36

Kim, Eun Sun, 176

Kincaid, Stacey, 158

Kitchen, Kristin, 268

Kress, Anne, 86

Lee, Esther, 68

MacLennan, Betsy, 22

Marshall, Cynthia, 234

McConnell, Megan, 10

Medina, Carmen, 120

O'Donnell, Norah, 135

Randhawa, Pam, 28

Reeves, Kathryne, 164

Ros-Lehtinen, Ileana, 124

Smith Spacek, Kimberly, 71

Snyder, Cora, 111

Strawderman, Lauren, 91

Thomas, Jakita Owensby, 250

Wallace, Margaret, 184

Walley, Tonya, 254

Wilson, Meredith, 228

Yasmin, Seema, 204

Endnotes

1   Rebecca Leppert and Drew Desilver, "118th Congress has a record number of women," Pew Research Center, January 3, 2023, https://www.pewresearch.org/fact-tank/2023/01/03/118th-congress-has-a-record-number-of-women/.

2   Emma Hinchliffe, "Women CEOs run more than 10% of Fortune 500 companies for first time in history," Fortune, January 12, 2023.

3   The Carta Team, "Annual equity report 2021," Carta.com.

4   "US VC female founders dashboard," PitchBook.com, January 5, 2023 and March 7, 2023.

5   Riddhi Setty, "US Women Represent 13% of US Patent Owners After 30 Years of Growth," Bloomberg Law, October 19, 2022.

6   Richard Fry, Brian Kennedy, and Cary Funk, "STEM Jobs See Uneven Progress in Increasing Gender, Racial and Ethnic Diversity," Pew Research Center, April 1, 2021.

7   "The Rise of the Virtual Empire: Video Game Industry Statistics," Fortunly, December 19, 2022

8   "A data-based look at America's physicians and medical students, state-by-state," Association of American Medical Colleges, January 13, 2022

9   U.S. Bureau of Labor Statistics, Job Outlook, September 8, 2022

10 BluePaper, Morgan Stanley Research, January 23, 2019, from full report, "Flying Cars: Investment Implications of Autonomous Urban Air Mobility," December 2, 2018.

Photo by Liz Ernest

About the Author

Julia Taylor Brandus, eleven, is a sixth grader in Virginia. She plays basketball and soccer, reads, and is learning to play the bass. She lives with her mom, dad, and Poppy the Corgi. This is her first book.